TAX Cafe™

Taxcafe.co.uk Tax Guides

Retire Rich with a Property Pension

By Nick Braun PhD

Important Legal Notices:

TAXCafe™

TAX GUIDE - "Retire Rich with a Property Pension"

Published by:
Taxcafe UK Limited
214 High St
Kirkcaldy KY1 1JT
Tel: (0044) 01592 560081
Email: team@taxcafe.co.uk

First Edition, November 2004
Second Edition, April 2005

ISBN 1 904608 25 6

About the Author and Taxcafe

Nick Braun founded Taxcafe.co.uk in Edinburgh in 1999, along with his partner Aileen Smith. As the driving force behind the company, their aim is to provide affordable plain-English tax information for investors, business owners, IFAs and accountants.

In the last five years Taxcafe.co.uk has become one of the best-known tax websites in the UK and received numerous accolades.

Nick has been involved in the tax publishing world since 1989 as a writer, editor and publisher. He holds a masters degree and doctorate in economics from the University of Glasgow, where he was awarded the prestigious William Glen Scholarship and later became a Research Fellow. Prior to that he graduated with distinction from the University of South Africa, the country's oldest university, earning the highest results in economics in the university's history.

He went on to become editor of *Personal Finance* and *Tax Breaks*, two of South Africa's best-known financial publications before moving to the UK.

Nick and Aileen are very keen property investors and own a large portfolio of buy-to-let flats in the Fife seaside town of Kirkcaldy where the Taxcafe head office is based.

When he's not working Nick likes to take his children to the zoo, relax with friends and eat good food.

Dedication

To Aileen for all your love and support over the years and to Jake, Sandy and Tilly for all the joy you've brought.

Nick Braun

Thanks

I'd like to thank all those who helped make Taxcafe possible. First and foremost, Martin Spring, founder of Prescon Publishing Corporation, for everything you taught me about writing, publishing and the world of business and economics.

Our tax experts, especially Carl Bayley for taking the plunge, David Collier, tax partner at Chiene & Tait, for being so generous with your time and Lee Hadnum for being such an enthusiastic member of the team.

The Taxcafe staff, Laura for your brilliant web design and creative skills, Aaron for your enthusiasm and remarkable technical knowledge and Gordon for helping keep the show on the road.

My advisers at Scottish Enterprise, especially Allan Mungall for telling us to "go for it", Sandy Findlay for helping move us forward and Alistair Gibb for your worldly counsel.

Contents

Introduction

As a property investor you have to make dozens of important decisions. The most important one is what I call the *where, what, when* decision – choosing where to invest, what type of property to go for in your chosen location and when is the best time to buy.

Of secondary importance, but still critical, is deciding *who* to use as your solicitor, mortgage provider and letting agent.

Then there's a host of minor decisions to make such as where to source affordable furnishings, how much decoration to do prior to letting, where to obtain buildings and contents insurance, and so on.

Ranking right up there beside *where, what, when* is your decision *how* to invest in property. By that I mean do you invest personally or by using some other legal structure? These are decisions made mainly to save tax.

Although saving tax should never be the main driving force behind your property investment, minimising tax is of critical importance. Get your tax planning wrong and you will end up paying a large proportion of your hard-earned profits to your silent partner, the taxman.

At present there are essentially three ways you can buy property:

- Personally,
- By setting up your own property company, or
- By setting up a property pension plan.

Most people invest personally which means they pay income tax on their rental income and capital gains tax when they sell property. Personal ownership is covered in detail in Carl Bayley's best-selling guide, *How to Avoid Property Tax.*

Investing through a company has become more and more popular in recent years as the company tax system has become more and more generous. As a general rule, property companies pay tax at much lower rates than personal investors, especially when all the profits are being reinvested, so using a company can be an extremely lucrative way to build a property portfolio over time. Property companies are covered in detail in our popular guide, *Using a Property Company to Save Tax.*

The third way you can buy property is through a self-invested personal pension (SIPP).

This is by far the most attractive way to protect your profits from the taxman and could have an enormous impact on the amount of wealth you can accumulate.

At present, however, property SIPPs are quite restrictive because they can only be used to buy *commercial property*. That's not necessarily a bad thing because commercial property is currently very much in vogue. However, most property investors would probably prefer to stick with what they know best, namely residential property.

Many investors are also put off pensions by other factors such as restrictions on how much can be invested and on how benefits can be taken when you retire.

The good news is that all this is about to change. From April 6th 2006 – known as A-Day in the pensions industry – we'll all be able to invest in residential property through our pension plans.

What's more, a whole bunch of other reforms will come into force that will make contributing to a pension plan more tax effective and more flexible than ever before.

Residential property pensions are the next 'big thing' in property investment. In fact, I would go so far as to say that residential property pensions will be as important as the invention of the buy-to-let mortgage.

From April 6th 2006 all property investors will have a very important decision to make every time they buy a property: should I buy personally or via a pension?

This guide will help you make this all-important decision and show you what to do in the months ahead.

In Chapter 1 I start off by taking a brief look at why investing in property is so popular and in Chapter 2 a brief overview is provided of the benefits and drawbacks of investing through a pension plan.

In Chapter 3 I take a detailed look at the tax reliefs available to pension savers. Using some interesting case studies, I will show how, by sheltering your investments in a pension plan, you could end up with between 50% and 140% more income.

In Chapter 4 I'll be looking at commercial property SIPPs: how they work, who offers them and why you should consider investing in one *now*.

Another important reason to read this chapter is so as to find out how SIPPs work in practice. A lot of investors focus too much attention on the Government's proposed pension changes and overlook the fact that, how residential property SIPPs will look, depends just as much on the SIPP providers – the companies offering the products.

Having a look at what is currently available from commercial property SIPP providers will give you some idea as to what will be available from residential property SIPP providers.

In Chapter 5 the A-Day pension changes are explained in plain English. I'll show you how tax relief on pension contributions will become possibly the most generous tax break around, how pension plans will become much more flexible and I'll be examining the new rules for investments in residential property.

In Chapter 6 I'll be using some case studies to determine *exactly* what you stand to gain at the end of the day by investing in residential property through a SIPP. Will it have an enormous effect on your ultimate investment income when all factors are taken into consideration? Read on and find out!

In Chapter 7 you'll find some guidance on what to do right NOW, either in preparation for the introduction of residential property SIPPs or to make the most of the current commercial property SIPP regime.

In Chapter 8 I take a look at another exciting new development for property investors: the launch of Real Estate Investment Trusts (also known as REITs). Reits are also likely to take the property investment world by storm when they're introduced. For the first time you'll be able to invest small amounts of money each month in residential or commercial property and spread your risk across a large portfolio of high-quality properties. I'll take a look at how they're likely to operate and the benefits and drawbacks of investing in them.

You'll also find a useful glossary at the back which explains some of the terminology used throughout the guide.

Thank you for purchasing this publication and I hope you find it useful.

Nick Braun, April 2005

Chapter 1

Why Property?

In Chapter 2 I'm going to provide a brief overview of the main benefits and drawbacks of investing in property through a pension plan. However, before that it's first important to answer the broader question: Why invest in property, especially now that prices have risen by so much?

Investors have become drawn to bricks and mortar in recent years by a variety of 'push factors' and 'pull factors'.

The most important push factor was the dismal performance of the stock market up until early 2003. Before the 'dot com' crash in 2000, share investment was all the rage and most investors enjoyed fantastic returns.

Share prices rose 200% during the Nineties with some technology shares achieving these gains in just days. It was an exciting time to invest and there was lots of talk about the 'new economy' – technologically driven and rewarding those investors who had the temerity to get in on the ground floor.

As the new millennium dawned, the Nasdaq (the leading US benchmark of tech companies) shattered the 5,000 barrier and investors set their sights on 6,000. Most were convinced the party would continue indefinitely and that shares weren't overpriced at all.

Soon, however, the dot commers started reporting massive losses and closing down and the Nasdaq began its infamous 80% slide into oblivion, dragging the share prices of all other companies around the globe with it.

It wasn't just the bursting of the dot com bubble that put so many people off stock market investment. The terrorist attacks on 'that day' and, more importantly, the Enron and other American financial scandals that followed, drove share prices down just as hard.

Figure 1
Property vs Shares
1996-2004

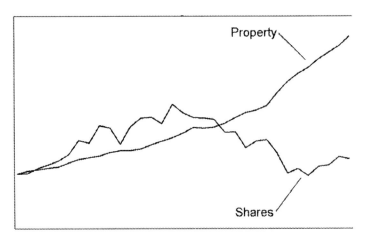

As always, when America sneezes the rest of the world catches a cold and by early 2003 the Footsie had lost a staggering 50% of its value. And remember the Footsie contains the very best companies. Those who bought tech shares and other small company shares lost most, if not all, of their money.

Cold percentages belie a very real human cost. Just think how a decline of that magnitude affects someone close to retirement. One day your pension fund is worth £500,000 and a short while later it's worth just £250,000. Needless to say, the dreams of many hard-working couples of an early or comfortable retirement were shattered by the stock market collapse.

It's hardly surprising then that so many ordinary savers and investors turned their backs on share investment and the City and started looking for alternative places to put their money.

The Pull Factors

It's pretty obvious why property investment has become so popular – returns have been spectacular over the years. You'll get a feel for this from Figure 1 which plots UK residential property prices from 1996 to early 2004. Over this time period a typical property grew in value from £51,367 to £149,742 – a rise of 192%! If you'd invested the same amount in shares you'd have benefited from a measly 19% return and your portfolio would be worth just £60,893.

Apart from enjoying tremendous capital growth, what has attracted many investors to property has been its low volatility. In other words, investors have not experienced massive knee-jerk increases or decreases in the value of their portfolios.

There's nothing worse than waking up on Monday morning and finding that 10% of your wealth has been wiped out. Share investors experience this sort of fright quite frequently, whereas property prices tend to change much more gently.

Although property investors have enjoyed spectacular returns in recent years, this is not a good enough reason to invest NOW. Many would argue that these years of exceptional property price inflation are over... and they're probably right.

But what's great about the 'buy-to-let model' is that you can enjoy impressive returns even when prices are only rising quite slowly.

To understand why, we have to take a closer look at some of the other pull factors for property investors.

Rental Income and Capital Growth

The great thing about investing in property is your returns come in two flavours: rental income and capital growth. For anyone lucky enough to own property outright this means you could earn something like 8% per year in rental income alone. So even if prices are rising only very gradually, say by 5% to 7% per year, you will still enjoy an impressive combined return.

Of course, very few investors own much property outright. It's different to virtually every other type of investment in that you usually have to borrow money to get in on the action. This is where one of the other pull factors comes into the picture.

Easy Mortgages & Low Interest Rates

Investing in property may require a large financial outlay but borrowing money to buy investment property has never been easier.

Have you ever noticed the signs in used-car sale-rooms that say "Guaranteed Finance"? Well it's pretty much like that in the mortgage lending market these days.

Until just a few years ago there were very few buy-to-let mortgages and the terms and conditions were pretty unappealing. In the last few years the market for buy-to-let mortgages has developed in leaps and bounds.

There's now so much competition that some fantastic deals are available. It's almost safe to say that banks and other lenders will lend large amounts of money to virtually anyone.

Apart from it being easy to borrow money, the cost of money is also extremely low. Even though interest rates have risen in recent times, they're still extremely low by historical standards, making it easy for many investors to buy property with borrowed money and meet the interest charges out of the rental income.

For example, the Bank of England base rate, which drives mortgage rates and other interest rates, has fallen from almost 14% in 1990 to around 5% today.

This brings us to the next pull factor for property investors, which makes investing still attractive when prices are only rising gradually.

The Power of Gearing – Turning 5% into 15%

We usually think of borrowing money as a negative – something you only do because you cannot afford to buy something outright. However, borrowing money to invest is something that even rich property investors do to turbo boost their returns.

Example

John has £20,000 to invest. He uses it as a deposit on a property costing £100,000 and borrows the rest. The property grows in value by a measly 5% per year over 10 years. Also, his rental income only covers the cost of his interest-only mortgage and his other letting costs – so all John is left with at the end of the day is the rise in the value of the property and his initial deposit.

After 10 years the property will be worth £163,000. If he sells it and repays his £80,000 loan he'll be left with £83,000. Despite only modest annual increases in property prices, John has managed to turn £20,000 into £83,000 in just 10 years. That means he has earned about 15% per year on his original money – a pretty impressive result.

This is the 'magic of gearing' and it is arguably the key to becoming wealthy through property.

So whether you buy property outright and enjoy both the capital growth and the rental income or borrow money and benefit from the capital growth on a much larger property, you can still make good money when property prices are only rising by a small amount.

This is the principle I use in all the case studies and examples in this guide. Nowhere is it automatically assumed that property prices will produce the spectacular returns we've witnessed in recent years.

Although the ability to gear property is one reason people are drawn to this investment, it is not necessarily why you would want to invest in a property *pension*. As we'll see in the chapters ahead, the new pension rules place a serious restriction on the amount that can be borrowed.

Bargains Are Easy to Find

One of the things I love most about property investment is that, unlike the stock market, genuine bargains can be had, provided you spend time acquiring the necessary local knowledge.

In other words, if you know what you're doing it's possible to find property selling for 'less that it should'.

This is rarely if ever possible with stock market investing. All the best deals and rich pickings are only every enjoyed by City traders and other professional investors. To use the correct investment jargon, the stock market is a much more 'efficient' market than the property market. Being 'inefficient' makes the property market far more attractive to amateur investors.

Also, with property it's much more easy to become a leading expert in one small area (for example, one *type* of property in one particular *location*) and reap significant rewards as a result. For example, I would say that my partner, Aileen Smith, knows as much as anyone about the market for two-bedroom flats in the town in which we live.

That's not an extravagant boast (the town in which we live is quite small) and I have no doubt that thousands of property investors can make similar claims. Having such 'insider knowledge' is one of the keys to making profitable property investments.

Now that we've looked at the advantages of investing in property generally, it's time to take a brief look at the benefits and drawbacks of investing through a pension plan.

Chapter 2

Property Pensions: Benefits and Drawbacks

Throughout this guide I'll be examining in detail the benefits and drawbacks of investing in property through a pension plan. This chapter contains a brief overview of the various advantages and disadvantages.

There is essentially only one benefit to be derived from making contributions to a pension plan:

Enormous tax savings

The drawbacks are far greater in number but (and it's a big 'but') taken together they probably do not outweigh the tremendous tax benefits.

Furthermore, some of the drawbacks will disappear when the new pension regime is introduced in April 2006.

Generous Tax Reliefs

When you contribute to a property pension plan (or any other type of pension plan) you are entitled to claim a series of tax reliefs including:

- Tax relief on your contributions – what I call buying property at a 40% discount.

- Tax-free investment returns – all your rental income and capital gains will be completely tax free.

- A tax-free lump sum when you retire.

In the next chapter I'll be taking a close look at how these tax reliefs operate and *exactly* how much they are worth to you at the end of the day.

To do this we'll follow the progress of two investors over many years, one investing inside a pension, the other investing outside a pension. I think you'll be surprised by the results.

Pension Drawbacks

Many of the pitfalls of investing in personal pensions, such as extortionate charges and limited investment flexibility, have been eradicated in recent years.

At present the three most serious drawbacks are that you lose access to your savings, are eventually forced to buy a fully taxed pension and have limited ability to leave your pension savings to your children and other relatives.

No Access to Your Money

This is one of the most serious drawbacks of investing in any pension plan. Once you hand over your money there's no chance of getting a refund. You will not be able to access any of your savings until you reach the minimum retirement age.

At present if you have a personal pension plan you can start withdrawing benefits from age 50 but from 2010 this age limit will, unfortunately, rise to 55.

What this means is that, no matter what financial storms blow across your decks between now and the day you reach the minimum age, your pension savings will not be there to bail you out.

There's not a lot I can say in defence of this rule. Although, it's not very pleasant losing access to your savings, the age rule shouldn't cause undue hardship to the majority of pension savers –

especially if the reason you're investing in property in the first place is to replace or supplement a traditional pension. For most property investors, pension planning *is* the primary motivation.

Furthermore, investing in a property pension is not an all-or-nothing decision. If you want to enjoy the best of both worlds (attractive tax breaks and access to your savings), you could keep some of your money tied up in traditional buy to let and some invested in a pension.

Compulsory Annuity

When you reach age 75 at the latest you currently have to use three-quarters of your pension savings to buy a pension for life, also known as a compulsory annuity. The problem with this rule is that:

- The annuity is fully taxed, and

- Annuity rates have fallen dramatically in recent years.

Of course, most other investment income is also fully taxed. The difference here, however, is that each annuity payment you receive consists of interest income *and* some of your original capital.

There is no other investment on the planet that taxes your original capital – that would be like putting your money in a bank account and paying tax on the whole lot, capital and interest, when you make a withdrawal.

In the previous chapter I mentioned the massive decline in share prices between 2000 and 2003. A less publicized but equally calamitous collapse has been the fall in annuity rates since the early 1980s.

The annuity rate is simply the amount of pension income £1 of savings can buy you. The annuity rate depends on your age and the level of interest rates. Because long-term interest rates in the

UK have been steadily falling since the 1970s, annuity rates have been falling as well. Interest rates peaked at about 15% in the early 1970s and have fallen to around 5% in recent years. Low interest rates have been great for the economy but have left a serious dent in the incomes of many retirees.

In 1980 the annuity rate was about 18%. By 2004 it had fallen to 7% – a fall of 60%. So if you had retirement savings of £250,000 in the early Eighties you would have received a pension of £45,000. If you retired with the same capital today you would receive just £17,500.

During the 1980s and 1990s this massive decline in interest rates was fantastic for share prices. Generally when interest rates fall the stock market rises. As a result many of those saving for retirement didn't notice or care too much about the drop in annuity rates. Falling interest rates may have affected final pension incomes but with share prices rising so fast most retirees were still better off.

However, when the big stock market collapse hit home, many retirement savers were left with two bitter pills to swallow: a halving of annuity rates <u>and</u> a halving of share prices, potentially leaving them with one quarter of the income they would have expected in an 'ideal world'.

It's not all doom and gloom, however.

Although the fall in annuity rates has been a painful side effect of investing through a pension, what this argument fails to recognize is that although interest rates and annuity rates have fallen dramatically in recent years, so too has inflation.

So while the initial income you receive from a pension annuity has fallen, the income you receive nowadays will hold on to its purchasing power for much longer.

Furthermore, from April 2006 you will no longer be forced to buy an annuity – a new and more flexible alternative is being introduced (see Chapter 5 for more information).

Nothing for the Kids

Another thing some people really hate about investing in traditional pensions is the fact that, when you die, your pension dies too and your heirs get nothing.

For example, Jimmy contributes to a pension fund for 40 years before retiring. His final pension pot is worth £500,000. Unfortunately, Jimmy and his wife die in an accident on the way home from the retirement do.

How much will their children inherit? Possibly not one penny is the simple answer.

Actuaries at the big life insurance companies explain that this outcome is totally fair. People who die young subsidize those who live longer than expected and everything balances out in the end. However, the investing public has never fully bought into this argument.

This is another reason many people saving for retirement want more control: control over how their savings are invested and control over what happens to their assets when they die.

Some of these problems will be partly fixed from April 6th 2006 and you may be able to pass on your pension savings to your family in certain circumstances.

Why Make Private Pension Provision?

While we're taking a broad look at pension benefits and drawbacks, it's also worth reiterating why it is so important to make your own private pension provision and not rely on the State or your employer's pension fund.

No Control Over How Your Savings Are Invested

Most pension fund members have absolutely no control over how their hard-earned savings are invested. If you work for a big company your pension contributions will disappear into a black hole and you'll probably have no idea what they're being invested in, who is managing your money and how well or badly they are performing.

I don't know about you but I don't find it very appealing having my savings and investments cloaked in such uncertainty.

Even if you have a personal pension you often won't know exactly what's going on if it's a run-of-the-mill personal pension. For example, your money might be invested in one of those mysterious with-profit funds in which you only earn what some insurance company actuary decides to pay you – 'without profits' is probably a more fitting name.

With self-invested personal pension plans, however, you will never face this problem. Most SIPP providers set up a bank account for you and let you track exactly how your investments are performing.

Withdrawal of Risk-free Final Salary Pensions

There are essentially two types of company pension scheme you can belong to: a 'final salary scheme' or a 'defined contribution scheme'.

Final salary schemes pay you a pension that has nothing to do with how well the stock market or other investments are performing or how much money your employer has contributed.

Your pension is dependent solely on your years of service and your final salary. For example, you may be entitled to 1/60th of your salary for each year you've worked for the company.

This type of scheme is quite cushy for employees because they are, in theory, completely protected from stock market crashes and bad investment decisions.

With defined contribution schemes, on the other hand, your employer promises to pay a 'defined contribution', eg 5% of your salary, into your pension fund. Your final pension then depends on how the pension fund's investments perform.

The crux is, final salary schemes are hated by employers, defined contribution schemes are hated by employees.

The good news for employers is that final salary schemes are being phased out and replaced with defined contribution schemes. The bad news for employees is that their pensions will in future depend mostly on stock market performance.

With this type of scheme the employer is essentially saying: "Here's some cash, we'll invest it for you. If it does well you'll have a good retirement income. If it doesn't, too bad."

Those who find this new arrangement unappealing will increasingly opt out and set up their own private pension plans.

Final Salary Schemes Won't Make You Rich Anyway

Even if you're lucky enough to belong to a final salary pension scheme, it's never going to make you rich.

Just think about it. You work for the same company for 20 years and end up on a salary of £60,000. How much pension will you receive? According to the normal formula, your pension will be a measly £20,000. Even if your children have flown the nest and you've paid off your home, that's hardly enough money for two people to retire on comfortably.

At the very most you'll be able to get by. And I don't think anyone reading this guide wants to simply 'get by'.

So even if you belong to a cushy final salary scheme you have to make extra retirement provision if you don't want to be hard up when you reach retirement age.

That's where a property pension could come in handy, as we'll see in the chapters that follow.

Pension Scandals

Over the last ten years a series of scandals, débâcles and outright scams have severely damaged the reputation of the financial services industry.

Perhaps the biggest crisis facing those saving for retirement is the underfunding of final salary pension funds.

When the stock market was riding high in the 1990s many companies took 'contribution holidays' and stopped paying money into their pension funds. Instead they relied on the rise in share prices to do their job for them.

When share prices collapsed a gaping hole emerged. Many pension funds now don't have enough money to meet their future commitments. Barely a day goes by when there isn't an article in the newspapers about a company with an underfunded pension fund.

If you work for a company in good financial shape you don't have to worry. The shareholders do, but not you. The company will simply top up the pension fund shortfall out of its profits. But if the company goes bankrupt and folds there'll be no one to make up the pension you're entitled to and you could walk away with nothing. This is a serious danger at present.

It shows that you cannot rely on your employer to secure your retirement. To guarantee a comfortable and prosperous retirement you have to take your financial planning into your own hands.

Chapter 3

The Amazing Pension Tax Reliefs

In the next few chapters I'm going to explain the tax benefits of investing in property through a self-invested personal pension (SIPP). We'll start in Chapter 4 by examining commercial property SIPPs because at present they're the only ones allowed by law.

However, from April 2006 it will be possible to put all sorts of investments into a SIPP, including houses and flats. And that's not the only exciting change taking place to the pension rules. There are lots of other important reforms that will make investing in a pension plan more attractive than ever before. In Chapter 5 I'll explain what these changes are and how they will help you with your property pension planning.

Then in Chapter 6 I'll take a really close-up look at the new residential property SIPPs and explain how they will work and illustrate in detail how they could revolutionize your property investing.

However, before taking a closer look at these issues it's essential to examine the pension tax reliefs in more detail.

Pensions truly are FANTASTIC tax shelters. Most of us have heard something about their tax benefits but up until now nobody has taken a *really* close look at just how powerful these tax concessions can be.

So that's what I decided to do in this book. Using my training as an economist, and armed with a whole bunch of spreadsheets, I decided to find out exactly how much better off you are investing through a pension compared with alternative investment routes.

I wanted to find out precisely how much more wealth you are likely to accumulate and how much more income you are likely to earn, if any, by investing through a pension plan.

The results make fascinating reading. They reveal some quite startling statistics about pensions that I have little doubt will prompt many readers to start using them more aggressively in their financial planning.

Far from being 'boring', pensions are one of the most powerful weapons in your financial armoury.

The generous tax reliefs are what make them so special and, as you'll see in the examples that follow, these reliefs could allow you to earn up to 140% more income than someone who decides to invest outside a pension. In other words, your investments could generate an annual income of £41,000 while your pension-shy friend could end up earning just £17,000.

Apart from the tax breaks, the other thing I love about pensions is that they're relatively cheap and easy to set up. What's more, unlike other tax shelters such as venture capital trusts and unlisted company shares, there is potentially very little risk involved. You can keep all your money invested in a bank account if you like!

Some readers might be asking, does he put his money where his mouth is? Well, after conducting the analysis that went behind this chapter I decided to *double* my personal pension contributions. And I'll increase them now whenever the opportunity arises.

After all, what could be more enticing than free cash? That's exactly what pensions offer you – the taxman's money and lots of it if you invest hard enough. It's like walking into the sales office at a new property development and saying: "Here's a cheque for 60% of the flat. The taxman's picking up the rest of the tab."

It sounds to good to be true but this fantastic state of affairs is just around the corner.

The Three Pension Tax Breaks

Pension plans live or die by their tax reliefs. Without them nobody would have any incentive to invest. In fact, without tax reliefs pension plans are lousy investments. Why? Because they lock your money away out of reach until you hit a certain age – 50 in the case of personal pensions.

Nobody likes losing control of their money unless there's a pretty big incentive for doing so. But as we'll see in this chapter, the tax reliefs ARE a big enough incentive.

So what are these tax reliefs, how do they work and how much are they really worth? That's what you'll find out in this chapter. What I won't get into here are all the nitty-gritty rules such as how much can be contributed each year and when and how benefits can be taken. That's important information but we'll leave it for later. It gets in the way of the really important issue which is whether you should invest in a pension in the first place!

There are three pension tax reliefs in total and they vary in importance. Let's examine each of them in turn.

Tax Relief #1 – Your Contributions

Free Pension Fund Top Ups – The First 22%

When you make pension contributions Inland Revenue will top up your savings by paying cash directly into your plan. Effectively for every £78 you invest, the taxman will put in an extra £22.

Why £22? Because your contributions are treated as having been paid out of income that has already been taxed at the basic income tax rate of 22%. The taxman is therefore refunding the income tax you've paid.

The pension scheme manager, usually an insurance company, will claim this money for you from Inland Revenue.

So whatever contribution you make, divide it by 0.78 and you'll get the TOTAL amount that is invested in your plan.

Example

Dave invests £100 per month in a personal pension. The total amount that will be invested, after the taxman makes his top-up payment, is:

£100/0.78 = £128

How valuable is this tax break compared with investing outside a pension plan? The best way of answering that is by means of an example.

Example

Amy invests in a personal pension. She starts by investing £3,900 and increases her investment by 3% per year. How much free cash will she get from the taxman?

In year one her total pension investment is:

£3,900/0.78 = £5,000

with £1,100 (£5,000 - £3,900) of that coming from the taxman. After 10 years, as her contributions increase, she'll have received a total of £12,610 in top-up contributions, after 20 years she'll have received £29,557 and after 30 years she'll have received a total of £52,333 from the taxman.

As we'll see later on in Chapter 5, Amy will be able to take all this free money and put it into exciting new residential property investments.

But this isn't necessarily the end of the story. If Amy is a *higher-rate* taxpayer, paying tax at 40%, she'll be able to claim even more tax relief.

The Cherry on Top – Higher Rate Relief

If you're a higher-rate taxpayer the taxman will let you claim the extra 18% (40% minus the 22% he's already given you) when you submit your tax return.

What's great about this relief is the money will not be paid into your pension plan which would mean your losing access to it until you retire. Instead you'll get a nice cheque in the post from the Inland Revenue. (Or if you haven't paid your taxes already, your tax bill will be reduced accordingly.)

Example

As we already know, Amy's personal contribution is £3,900 and total pension fund investment, including the taxman's contribution, is:

£3,900/0.78 = £5,000.

The £3,900 is what's known as her 'net contribution' and the £5,000 is what's known as her 'gross contribution'. Multiplying her gross contribution by 18% (40% – 22%) we get:

£5,000 x 18% = £900

This is the amount of tax that will be refunded to Amy.

Effectively she has a pension investment of £5,000 which has cost her just £3,000 (£3,900 personal contribution less her £900 refund). In other words, she's getting all her investments at a 40% discount.

This is the critical number. Being able to make investments year after year at a 40% discount can have a massive effect on the amount of wealth you can accumulate. It's a no-brainer when you think about it.

Over a long period of time how much tax is Amy likely to save thanks to higher-rate relief?

Example

Just as before let's assume Amy starts by investing £3,900 and increases her investment by 3% per year. How much tax relief will she get over the years if she's a higher-rate taxpayer?

After 10 years she'll have personally contributed £44,709 into her pension plan and this will have been topped up by £12,610 from the taxman. She'll also have received tax refunds of £10,317. Her total tax relief is £22,927.

After 20 years she'll have received £53,741 in tax relief and, after 30 years, a whopping £95,151.

Summary

- When you make pension contributions you qualify for two different types of tax relief: Basic-rate tax relief which comes in the shape of top-ups to your pension plan and higher-rate relief which takes the shape of a tax refund paid to you personally.

- Your total pension fund investment is found by dividing your personal contribution by 0.78. The excess is paid by the taxman to your pension provider.

- Higher-rate relief is calculated by multiplying your gross pension fund contribution by 18%.

- Together they mean all your pension investments come in at a 40% discount.

- Although basic-rate relief is paid directly into your pension fund and is out of reach until you arrive at the minimum retirement age, it's important to stress that the money is yours to invest as you please. Most personal pension plans these days, especially SIPPs, give you enormous investment flexibility.

- With higher-rate relief you don't have to use the tax refund to make other investments, although this would be the sensible thing to do. You can do whatever you like with it: go on holiday, pay off some of your mortgage or buy a new car.

Tax Break #2 – Tax-free Investment Returns

Your money's sitting in a pension plan with an extra top-up of 22% from the taxman. What now?

Apart from obtaining tax relief on your contributions, all your pension savings are now allowed to grow completely free from income tax and capital gains tax.

This is potentially an extremely valuable tax break and could have an enormous effect on the amount of capital you are able to accumulate. And the more capital you accumulate, the higher your final pension income.

Remember the returns from most investments such as property, shares, bank interest and bonds are taxed at rates as high as 40%, so a concession like this is extremely valuable.

To see just how important this tax break is, let's take a look at an example. For now we'll ignore the fact that pension contributions qualify for tax relief and focus solely on the tax-free investment growth.

Example

Kwame invests £5,000 per year in a pension and enjoys tax-free investment growth of 7% per year. He increases the amount he invests by 3% per year.

Katrina also invests £5,000 per year in an investment that grows by 7% per year but she pays 40% tax on her returns. For example, she could be earning property rents or investing in corporate bonds or even one of the new real estate investment trusts (REITs) that will be on the investment menu soon (see Chapter 8).

How do Kwame's and Katrina's returns compare? They're both contributing exactly the same amount and earning identical pre-tax returns. *So any difference is down to tax treatment alone.*

The results are summarised in Table 1. At the end of year one Kwame has his £5,000 investment plus a tax-free return of 7% which comes to £5,350 in total. Katrina has her £5,000 investment plus an after-tax return of just 4.2%. So she is left with just £5,210 at the end of the year.

Table 1
Taxed vs Tax-Free Investment Growth

End Yr	Kwame	Katrina	% Diff
1	5,350	5,210	3
2	11,235	10,795	4
3	17,697	16,776	5
4	24,782	23,173	7
5	32,538	30,011	8
6	41,018	37,311	10
7	50,278	45,099	11
8	60,377	53,401	13
9	71,381	62,244	15
10	83,358	71,656	16
11	96,383	81,667	18
12	110,535	92,309	20
13	125,900	103,614	22
14	142,570	115,617	23
15	160,642	128,353	25
16	180,222	141,861	27
17	201,423	156,180	29
18	224,366	171,351	31
19	249,179	187,417	33
20	276,003	204,425	35
21	304,986	222,420	37
22	336,287	241,454	39
23	370,079	261,578	41
24	406,543	282,847	44
25	445,876	305,317	46
26	488,289	329,049	48
27	534,007	354,105	51
28	583,272	380,550	53
29	636,341	408,453	56
30	693,493	437,886	58

At the end of year two Kwame has his £5,350 from last year *plus* tax-free growth on that money, plus this year's investment *plus* tax-free growth on that money. In total he now has £11,235 compared with Katrina's £10,795.

And so it goes on, year after year, with Kwame enjoying tax-free growth and Katrina paying 40% of her returns to the taxman. Eventually after 10 years Kwame has £11,702 more than Katrina, after 20 years he has £71,578 more than her and after 30 years he has an incredible £255,607 more!

The fourth column in the table shows us how much better off Kwame is proportionately. After the first couple of years the difference is very small and Kwame has just 4% more money than Katrina. But the difference grows year after year until after 30 years Kwame is left with an impressive 58% more money than Katrina and all thanks to his decision to invest through a pension plan.

The reason Kwame becomes proportionately more wealthy with every year that passes is thanks to the 'magic' of compound interest. Every year he earns more money on every pound of his savings and reinvests those extra profits. Those extra profits in turn generate tax-free profits which are reinvested... and so on.

Compound interest is a great friend of pension savers, especially those with an eye to the long term.

Summary

- Pensions offer tax-free investment returns. This is potentially an extremely valuable tax break and could be worth tens of thousands of pounds to you over the long term.
- After 10 years you could have 16% more money than someone who pays tax on their profits, after 20 years you could have 35% more money and after 30 years you could have 58% more money.
- The longer you save, the more you will benefit from this tax break.

Putting the Two Tax Reliefs Together

So far we've seen that by contributing to a pension you can enjoy a 40% discount on your investments. We've also seen that once your money is inside a pension plan it can grow tax free and this could have an enormous effect on the amount of wealth accumulated.

Both of these pension tax breaks are clearly attractive in their own right. But what happens when you put them together?

Well then you have a truly powerful cocktail of tax savings!

The tax savings are so large that one wonders why anyone wouldn't make the maximum possible contribution into a personal pension. It could be the difference between a very ordinary and a very prosperous retirement.

What we'll do in this section is track two investors, Donald and Warren, over the next 30 years, each of them making identical investments and earning identical returns. The only difference is that Donald will invest in a pension; Warren will invest outside a pension.

You will see that after just 10 years Donald, the pension investor, will have accumulated almost twice as much money as Warren. And after 30 years Donald is in a completely different league. His savings will have grown to £693,493, whereas Warren will have just £262,732.

Let's take a closer look at how this amazing result is obtained.

Example - Donald and Warren

At the beginning of the year Donald invests £3,900 in his personal pension plan. The taxman adds another £1,100 bringing his total investment to £5,000. Donald is a successful estate agent and is therefore a higher-rate taxpayer. As a result he claims an extra £900 per year in tax relief. So he has acquired £5,000 of investments for just £3,000. He increases his pension contribution by 3% per year and the money in the pension plan grows by 7% per year.

Donald's friend Warren holds down a successful job in the City and is also a higher-rate taxpayer. He's a bit sceptical about pensions and decides not to use one. We'll assume Warren invests £3,000 per year (which is exactly how much Donald invests out of his own pocket). Warren also earns 7% per year but, because he pays tax at 40%, earns only 4.2% per year on his investments.

The two scenarios are summarised in Table 2.

At the end of year one Donald has pension savings of £5,000 plus tax-free growth at 7% which comes to £5,350. Warren, on the other hand has savings of £3,000 and investment growth of 4.2% which comes to £3,126. Already after just one year Donald has 71% more money than Warren!

At the end of year two Donald has earned another 7% on the £5,350 from last year which comes to £5,724.50. Plus he's made a fresh contribution of £5,150 and earned 7% on that which comes to £5,510.50. In total his savings are now worth £11,235.

And what about the hapless Warren? At the end of year two he has earned another 4.2% on the £3,126 from last year and has made a fresh contribution of £3,090 and earned 4.2% on that. In total his savings are worth £6,477.

And so the process continues with Donald becoming proportionately richer than Warren with every year that passes. After 10 years he has 94% more money than Warren, after 20 years he has 125% more money and after 30 years he has 164% more money.

Donald is becoming richer because every year he is investing more than Warren and every year he is earning higher after-tax returns. These higher returns are themselves reinvested tax free to produce even higher returns the following year.

Table 2
Taxed vs Tax-Free Investment Growth

End year	Pension	No Pension	% Diff
1	5,350	3,126	71
2	11,235	6,477	73
3	17,697	10,065	76
4	24,782	13,904	78
5	32,538	18,006	81
6	41,018	22,387	83
7	50,278	27,059	86
8	60,377	32,040	88
9	71,381	37,346	91
10	83,358	42,993	94
11	96,383	49,000	97
12	110,535	55,385	100
13	125,900	62,168	103
14	142,570	69,370	106
15	160,642	77,012	109
16	180,222	85,117	112
17	201,423	93,708	115
18	224,366	102,810	118
19	249,179	112,450	122
20	276,003	122,655	125
21	304,986	133,452	129
22	336,287	144,872	132
23	370,079	156,947	136
24	406,543	169,708	140
25	445,876	183,190	143
26	488,289	197,429	147
27	534,007	212,463	151
28	583,272	228,330	155
29	636,341	245,072	160
30	693,493	262,732	164

Tax Break #3 – Tax-free Lump Sum

It's now time for Donald to start benefiting from all this money he has been accumulating in his pension plan.

It's important to stress that 'retiring' from your pension plan does not mean you have to dig out your slippers and read the newspaper all day!

Maybe you want to leave your current job and do something completely different such as have a career change or start a business. Having a wad of cash and a regular pension income will make this a lot easier and less stressful.

This is where the final pension tax relief comes in handy. When you cash in your pension savings you can take 25% as a tax-free lump sum. This lump sum can be put to a number of good uses. You could use it to buy a rental property to boost your retirement income or to pay off mortgage debt on other buy-to-let properties that you hold personally. Or you could use it to fund a new business... or just blow it on holidays and having a good time!

The Sting in the Tail...

Although you can take one quarter of your savings as a tax-free lump sum the rest ultimately has to be used to buy what is known as a 'compulsory annuity' – which is just actuary speak for monthly pension.

(As it happens you don't necessarily have to buy an annuity immediately. SIPP investors can wait until they reach 75 and benefit from 'income drawdown' in the meantime. This lets you extract just the income from your pension savings, leaving the rest to accumulate tax-free until you wish to retire properly. More about this in Chapter 5.)

Although there has been tax relief on everything so far (contributions, investment growth and your lump sum), the annuity is *fully taxed*. And there's a massive difference between the tax treatment of compulsory pension annuities and virtually every other form of investment income.

The difference is that you are taxed on both your interest AND your capital.

When you hand over your pension savings to buy the annuity, the life insurance company invests it in low-risk Government bonds and pays you a monthly income. The income consists of the interest on the bonds *plus* a little bit of your original capital.

By paying you back some of your capital each month your income will be higher than that available from most other investments which only pay interest. This is one of the major benefits of annuities.

What's more, the payments are guaranteed to continue for life, whether you live for another three years or another 50 years! You don't have to worry about running out of savings.

While receiving capital repayments each month is a good way of boosting your retirement income, having to pay tax on them is a distinct disadvantage. That's equivalent to putting £100 in a bank deposit and paying £40 in tax when you withdraw the money a year later.

Of course this is not what happens with your bank savings in practice. You only pay tax on the *interest* you earn (a couple of pounds probably) and your capital will be paid back in full with no further tax liability.

So while there are tremendous tax benefits to investing in pension plans there is also a major tax penalty at the end.

The critical question is, do the upfront tax benefits – tax relief on contributions, tax-free investment growth and a tax-free lump sum – outweigh the penalty of the fully taxed pension income at the end?

This is the all-important question and I'm going to answer it shortly. However, to do that it's first important to explain why annuities are so important in pension planning, how they work in practice and the difference between compulsory and purchased annuities.

Why Annuities are So Important

Before you roll over and switch off the light I must warn you that this is an important section of the guide. Why? Because the humble annuity is fundamental to a lot of successful pension planning.

Some of the most interesting chapters in this guide are the ones that compare returns from property pensions with direct property investments. These chapters are designed to help you make important long-term investment decisions.

For example, do the fantastic tax reliefs available from pension products make them significantly more attractive than conventional property investments? Or should you just carry on with traditional buy to let?

Annuities are fundamental to these case studies because the verdict in favour of any type of investment is based solely on the amount of *income* it pays you at the end of the day.

If you have a property SIPP, or any other pension, this all-important final income will probably come in the shape of an annuity.

Even if you are doing your property pension planning *outside* a pension plan you may still want to buy an annuity one day with some or all of your capital.

And to make sure I'm comparing apples with apples this is exactly what I assume the investors in my examples do when they wish to retire: they sell all their property and other investments and buy an annuity.

If the investor who uses a property pension plan ends up with a much higher after-tax annuity income than the traditional property investor then the conclusion is that pensions are better investments.

But before you move on to the different case studies I want to make sure you have a solid understanding of the annuity concept so that the examples that follow make easy reading.

What is an Annuity?

Let's say you have a lump sum of £100,000 and want to use it to boost your retirement income. You're not too bothered about leaving any of the money to your heirs: your priority is maximizing your retirement income.

You could invest the money in property to earn rental income, shares to earn dividends or a bank or bonds to earn interest. The problem with these investments is they leave your capital intact, whereas, if maximizing your income is the priority, what you really should be doing is dipping into your capital as well.

(This is the type of tough decision that many investors with inadequate pension savings will be making more and more often in the years ahead. Many retirees will be forced to dip into their capital to obtain a large enough pension income.)

This is the advantage of annuities. Each payment consists of interest income and some of your original capital. As a result, the income is often far higher than income from other investments.

Of course spending your capital would be extremely risky if you went it alone and set up your own 'DIY annuity'. Certainly your heirs would inherit whatever was left over but what would you do if you lived to a ripe old age and exhausted your capital before you died?

This problem never affects annuity investors because their income is guaranteed for life. The big insurance companies do this by 'pooling mortality risk'. In other words, people who die younger

34

subsidize those that live longer. Sounds horrible doesn't it? Nevertheless it works and could ensure you have a very comfortable retirement.

What most people don't like about annuities is that when you die so too does your pension. Your heirs generally get nothing. However, there is a misconception among many savers that if you die early your surplus annuity capital goes into the life insurance company's coffers.

This is actually not the case. The money is used to pay the pensions of those who live longer and who end up getting significantly more income than they originally paid in.

This is the key benefit of annuities. They protect you against one of the greatest uncertainties of all: how long you will live. They do this by redistributing income from those who die younger to those who die older.

The amount of annuity income you get will depend on a variety of factors. The most important ones are your age (the older you are the higher the income), your sex (women live longer so get less income) and the current level of interest rates (the insurer will invest your money in government bonds that earn interest so the higher the level of interest rates the higher your annuity income).

There are a number of bolt-ons that will also affect the level of your annuity income. The most important one is inflation protection. Inflation protection means your initial income will be lower but increase in line with the retail prices index.

It's a must-have because even low inflation slowly eats into the purchasing power of your savings over time. Even growth assets such as property and shares cannot guarantee a gradually rising income over time.

Pension vs Purchased Annuities

There are essentially two types of annuity:

- Pension or compulsory annuities. This is the type of annuity you buy with your pension plan savings.

- Purchased or voluntary annuities. This is the type of annuity anyone with a lump sum can buy.

With both types of annuity all you have to do is give an insurance company a lump sum and it will pay you a monthly income for life.

The monthly payment will include interest and a bit of your original capital.

There are, however, two major differences between the two different types of annuity:

- Purchased annuities pay less income than pension annuities because the market for them is less competitive and because people who volunteer to buy them generally live longer than average.

- Although purchased annuities pay less income, unlike pension annuities, the capital portion of your income is *completely tax free*. As a result, the after-tax income from purchased annuities is often much higher than from other investments.

Although the annuity you receive depends primarily on your age, sex and the level of interest rates, annuity rates vary significantly from insurer to insurer, depending on how eager these companies are to attract this type of business.

The Financial Services Authority (FSA) produces a useful comparison of annuity quotes on its website:

http://www.fsa.gov.uk/tables

At the time of writing this guide, one of the insurance companies offering the most competitive annuity rates was Friends Provident.

So I asked them to provide me with some sample quotes. These are contained in Table 3.

As you can see, the compulsory annuity income is quite a bit higher than the purchased annuity income. However, most of the purchased annuity income comes in the form of capital repayment and is therefore completely tax free.

For example, if the person receiving the compulsory annuity is a basic-rate taxpayer his after-tax income will be £5,824 (£7,280.40 minus 20% tax) compared with £6,590 from a purchased annuity.

And if the person receiving the compulsory annuity is a higher-rate taxpayer his after-tax income will be £4,368 compared with £6,360 from a purchased annuity.

Clearly purchased annuities are a powerful way of generating income, especially if you manage to retire when interest rates are quite high. Earning £6,360 per year after tax on an investment of £100,000 is equivalent to earning 10.6% from a regular bank account.

Back now to Donald and Warren to see who ends up better off on retirement.

Donald and Warren – The Final Outcome

Just to recap, in the previous example Donald (investing in a pension) and Warren (not using a pension) ended up with the following savings after different time periods.

	Donald £	Warren £
After 5 years	32,538	18,006
After 10 years	83,358	42,993
After 15 years	160,642	77,012
After 20 years	276,003	122,655
After 25 years	445,876	183,190
After 30 years	693,493	262,732

Table 3
Annual Annuity Rates

Male age 65 with £100,000
Annual income, no inflation protection

Compulsory annuity	**£7,280.40**
Purchased Annuity	**£6,819.96**

Of which:

Tax-free capital portion	£5,671
Taxable interest portion	£1,148.96

Source: Friends Provident

We know that Donald has significantly higher pension savings than Warren but what happens when both investors start using their savings to produce income. How much better off is Donald then?

This is the crux of the matter because, after all, the only reason to invest in a pension fund is to ultimately provide a secure income when you retire.

So the true benefit of investing in pensions will only be revealed when we compare Donald's final income with Warren's final income.

However, to make sure we're comparing apples with apples it's essential to assume that both investors put their money into income-producing investments that are as near as possible identical.

Donald is forced to buy a pension annuity with three-quarters of his savings. With the remaining 25% he can do as he pleases.

Warren can do what he wants with all of his money. However, if we assume that he invests in, say, rental property, bank deposits or shares, we will not be comparing apples with apples.

It is impossible to compare Donald's annuity with any other form of investment income. Annuities have the following attractive features that other investments cannot boast:

- They are paid every month without fail until you die. You cannot be 100% certain that property or virtually any other asset will produce income every month for the rest of your life.

- You know exactly *how much* income your annuity will pay you every month. The same cannot be said of property, shares and other assets. And if you go for inflation protection you know exactly how much your income will grow.

- Your annuity pays you back some of your capital each month, providing a further boost to your income. With other assets you generally have to keep your capital intact. For example, you cannot sell a few thousand pounds' worth of property each year and use the money to live off.

So to ensure that Donald and Warren are investing in comparable income-producing assets we have to assume that Warren also buys an annuity with all his savings. Because he hasn't been investing in a pension, Warren will have to buy a 'purchased annuity'.

We'll assume that Donald and Warren take their savings and do the following:

- Donald uses 75% of his savings to buy a compulsory annuity for life.
- Donald uses his 25% tax-free lump sum to buy a purchased annuity for life.
- Warren uses all his savings to buy a purchased annuity for life.

I'll use the annuity quotes from Friends Provident (see Table 3) and assume both Donald and Warren are 65 when they decide to retire. The final income calculation is contained in Table 4.

At the end of the day Donald ends up with income of £41,717 compared with Warren's £17,314.

Put another away, Donald's pension income is almost two and a half times as much as Warren's.

This result is staggering and shows the true power of the pension tax break. Remember Donald and Warren made *identical investments* each year and earned *identical pre-tax returns*.

The only difference is Donald put his money in a pension plan while Warren invested outside a pension.

This result proves that pensions should be used by everybody investing for retirement.

Some investors dislike having to lock their savings away until they reach the minimum retirement age. This is a valid criticism. However, in my opinion, the tax benefits far outweigh this lack of flexibility.

Table 4
Final Income Comparison

Donald's Income Calculation After 30 Years

Pension Annuity:

	£
Total pension savings	693,493
75% Pension Annuity Purchase	520,120
Annual Annuity @ £7,280.40 per £100,000	37,865
Less tax @ 20% savings rate	**30,292**

Purchased Annuity

Lump sum - 25% of £693,493	173,373
Annual Annuity @ £6,819.96 per £100,000	11,824

Of which:

Tax-free capital portion	9,832
Taxable interest portion	1,992
Less tax @ 20%	398
Total Purchased Annuity Income	**11,426**

Total Pension Income	**41,717**

Warren's Income Calculation After 30 Years

Purchased Annuity

Total savings	262,732
Annual Annuity @ £6,819.96 per £100,000	17,918

Of which:

Tax-free capital portion	14,900
Taxable interest portion	3,019
Less tax @ 20%	604

Total Purchased Annuity Income	**17,314**

Note: Assumption is Donald and Warren are basic-rate taxpayers when they retire and pay tax at 20% on their pensions.

Shorter Savings Periods

The above example showed final income after 30 years. This may sound like a long time but it's not really. That's equivalent to starting investing at the age of 35, which is not an unreasonable age to start contributing to a pension plan. Many investors start contributing earlier.

However, for those with a shorter time horizon it's important to show how the pension vs non-pension results compare if we assume savings take place for a much shorter period of time.

For example, if you're 50 years old now you've only got another 15 years to make pension contributions. Is the pension route still as profitable?

The answer, in a nutshell, is yes.

Table 5 shows the final retirement incomes of Donald, the pension plan saver, and Warren, the non-pension saver, over a range of time periods.

In this table we're assuming that there are lots of Donalds and Warrens of different ages! One pair reaches age 65 after saving for five years, one pair reaches age 65 after saving for 10 years and the final pair reaches age 65 after saving for 30 years.

Income is calculated in exactly the same way as in Table 4.

The results speak for themselves. The shorter the time period the smaller the gap between the two savers. However, even over short time periods Donald, the pension saver, still ends up with a lot more income than Warren.

Even after contributing to a pension plan for just five years Donald still ends up with 65% more income.

So even if you don't have a very long investment horizon, investing through a pension plan should feature high on your list of priorities.

Table 5
Retirement Income over Different Time Periods

	Donald	**Warren**	**% Difference**
After 5 years	1,957	1,187	65
After 10 years	5,014	2,833	77
After 15 years	9,664	5,075	90
After 20 years	16,603	8,083	105
After 25 years	26,822	12,073	122
After 30 years	41,717	17,314	141

Basic-rate Taxpayers

So far we've shown how a *higher-rate* taxpayer can earn a much higher retirement income by contributing to a pension plan. Higher-rate taxpayers are those earning more than £37,295 per year. What about those who earn less. Are pensions still attractive to basic-rate taxpayers?

The only way to find out is by following another two investors over the course of their working lives. We'll use exactly the same methods as before so we can fast track the process and get straight to the results.

Example
David and Michael are great footballers. Although they had dreams of making it big they never quite managed to pull it off. Both now teach PE at the local comprehensive.

They're quite frugal with their spending and decide to start saving £3,000 per year for retirement. David has a razor sharp mind for figures and decides to save through a pension. Michael, on the other hand, decides to save outside a pension. David's total pension investment in year one will be £3,846 after the taxman has topped it up (£3,000/0.78). Michael's total investment will be just £3,000.

Again we assume that both of them earn 7% per year which means Michael will earn just 5.6% after paying tax at 22%. They also increase their contributions by 3% per year.

Table 6 tracks their progress over the years. At the end of year one both have savings equal to their initial investments (£3,846 or £3,000) plus growth on that money (7% and 5.6% respectively). At the end of year two they've made fresh contributions and earned growth on their existing contributions... and so the process continues.

The fourth column shows how much better off David is than Michael. The difference is not as extreme as between Donald and Warren, the higher-rate taxpayers, but is still quite substantial.

After 10 years good old David has 38% more money than Michael, after 20 years he has almost 50% more money and after 30 years he has 62% more money.

And how do they fare when they start drawing income at age 65? As before we'll assume that David uses 75% of his pension savings to buy a pension annuity and takes the rest as a tax-free lump sum and uses it to buy a purchased annuity. Michael uses all his savings to buy a purchased annuity.

The after-tax incomes they both receive are summarised in Table 7.

Once again the results speak loud and clear. No matter how long David invests he earns significantly more income than Michael. Even after just five years David is 22% better off.

Clearly basic-rate taxpayers should also consider saving as much as possible through a pension.

Table 6
Pension vs Non-pension Returns
Basic-rate Taxpayers

End Year	Pension	No Pension	%Diff
1	4,115	3,168	30
2	8,642	6,608	31
3	13,613	10,339	32
4	19,063	14,380	33
5	25,030	18,751	33
6	31,552	23,474	34
7	38,675	28,571	35
8	46,444	34,067	36
9	54,908	39,988	37
10	64,121	46,361	38
11	74,141	53,215	39
12	85,027	60,580	40
13	96,846	68,489	41
14	109,669	76,977	42
15	123,571	86,080	44
16	138,633	95,836	45
17	154,941	106,286	46
18	172,589	117,475	47
19	191,676	129,446	48
20	212,310	142,251	49
21	234,604	155,938	50
22	258,683	170,564	52
23	284,676	186,186	53
24	312,725	202,865	54
25	342,982	220,665	55
26	375,607	239,655	57
27	410,775	259,908	58
28	448,671	281,500	59
29	489,493	304,512	61
30	533,456	329,031	62

Table 7
Pension vs Non-pension Returns
Basic-rate Taxpayers

	Pension	No Pension	% Diff
After 5 years	1,506	1,236	22
After 10 years	3,857	3,055	26
After 15 years	7,433	5,673	31
After 20 years	12,772	9,375	36
After 25 years	20,632	14,542	42
After 30 years	32,090	21,684	48

Pensions vs ISAs

Those with a reasonable knowledge of tax law may not like one of the assumptions I made early on.

In the examples so far I've assumed that the person investing outside a pension pays tax on his returns *every year*.

This is a valid assumption when you're looking at rental or dividend income or interest from bonds or bank deposits. However, it would not be totally valid when it comes to that part of your investment returns that comes from capital growth, such as from rising property prices.

Capital gains are not taxed when you earn them. Tax only comes into the picture when you *sell* the asset.

Furthermore, capital gains are taxed much more leniently than other forms of investment return. If you hold on to your investments for more than 10 years you'll only pay tax on 60% of your profits. And you'll also be able to reduce the taxable amount by your annual capital gains tax exemption (currently £8,500 per person).

So if Warren and Michael, the non-pension savers in the above examples, have earned a lot of their returns from capital growth, it's unfair to assume that they pay tax on their returns every year. Doing so understates their returns and overstates the tax benefits of investing through a pension.

To fix this problem let's be ultra generous to Warren and Michael and assume that they **never pay any tax on their investment returns** and see how they perform compared with Donald and David who invest through a pension plan.

Doing so will provide an important additional insight. If you invest in an individual savings account (ISA) you pay no tax on your investment returns, so by assuming that Warren and Michael pay no tax on their investment returns we are in effect comparing the tax benefits of investing in a personal pension with the tax benefits of investing in an ISA.

Pensions and ISAs are the best-known investment tax shelters. I've read lots of articles comparing their benefits and drawbacks but most, including those written by investment professionals, are a bit superficial.

Amazingly, nobody has taken a really detailed look at which investment offers superior tax breaks. That's what we're going to do in this section. I'm going to show you that ISAs are simply nowhere near as powerful as pensions.

The main similarities and differences can be summarised as follows:

- Like pensions, ISAs offer tax-free investment growth. Furthermore, any income you withdraw is completely tax free. When you cash in your ISA there is no further tax charge.

- Pensions offer up-front tax relief which means you could end up getting all your investments at a 40% discount. However, when you start withdrawing benefits you ultimately have to buy an annuity with 75% of your savings and pay tax on both your income and capital.

- ISAs are extremely flexible investments that allow you to access your savings at any time. Pension benefits can only be withdrawn from age 50.

- ISAs cannot be used to invest directly in property. As we'll see in the next chapter, pensions can currently be used to invest in commercial property and from 2006 in residential property.

- The maximum annual ISA investment is £7,000 per person. The maximum personal pension investment is currently between £18,480 and £42,240 per year, depending on your age. From 2006 the maximum investment will be 100% of your earnings up to £215,000.

- The long-term future of ISAs is uncertain. Although the current annual investment limits were extended to 2010 in the 2005 Budget, there's no knowing what will happen after that date.

The all-important question is, how do ISAs compare with pensions pound for pound? Which is the more powerful tax-planning tool?

Time for another example!

Example
Hugo and Alan, both higher-rate taxpayers, each want to invest £3,000 per year.

Hugo uses a personal pension plan. He makes an initial contribution of £3,900 to which the taxman adds a further £1,100 in tax relief. He then claims back £900 when completing his tax return.

All in all he has £5,000 of investments which have only cost him £3,000.

Alan goes for an ISA and invests £3,000 per year. He doesn't get any tax relief on his contributions but, like Hugo, his investment returns are all completely tax free. Both earn 7% per year.

We track how they're doing from year to year in Table 8 (we're assuming here that ISAs will still be available after 2010).

Hugo gets out of the blocks much faster than Alan and after just one year already has £2,140 more savings: £2,000 in tax relief and £140 investment growth on that tax relief.

After five years he has £32,538 compared with Alan's £19,523; after 10 years he has £33,343 more than Alan; after 20 years he has £110,401 more than Alan and after 30 years he has £277,397 more money.

So even though they're both earning identical tax-free investment returns Hugo is much better off than Alan. This is because his annual investment is much higher thanks to tax relief on his contributions and those contributions in turn are growing within the fund.

However, the really important comparison will be their final pension incomes.

Again we assume that Hugo uses 75% of his savings to buy a pension annuity and uses his tax-free lump sum to buy a purchased annuity. Alan uses all his ISA savings to buy a purchased annuity, with most of the income tax free.

The results are summarised in Table 9.

As with all the examples we've looked at so far the pension investor comes out on top. Hugo earns 52% more income than Alan whether he invests for just five years or 30 years.

And 52% is a lot of money. For example, after 30 years Hugo will be earning £41,717 compared with Alan's £27,421.

Admittedly the difference is not as extreme as in the example of Donald and Warren. However, it's enough to allow us to draw the conclusion that pension plans are the most lucrative way of accumulating wealth.

Table 8
Pension Returns vs ISA Returns

End Yr	Pension	ISA
1	5,350	3,210
2	11,235	6,741
3	17,697	10,618
4	24,782	14,869
5	32,538	19,523
6	41,018	24,611
7	50,278	30,167
8	60,377	36,226
9	71,381	42,828
10	83,358	50,015
11	96,383	57,830
12	110,535	66,321
13	125,900	75,540
14	142,570	85,542
15	160,642	96,385
16	180,222	108,133
17	201,423	120,854
18	224,366	134,619
19	249,179	149,507
20	276,003	165,602
21	304,986	182,991
22	336,287	201,772
23	370,079	222,047
24	406,543	243,926
25	445,876	267,526
26	488,289	292,974
27	534,007	320,404
28	583,272	349,963
29	636,341	381,805
30	693,493	416,096

Table 9
Final Income: Pension vs ISA

	Pension	ISA	% Difference
After 5 years	1,957	1,287	52
After 10 years	5,014	3,296	52
After 15 years	9,664	6,352	52
After 20 years	16,603	10,913	52
After 25 years	26,822	17,630	52
After 30 years	41,717	27,421	52

Summary

- In this chapter I've tried to show exactly how valuable the pension tax break is. This is very important for anyone wanting to invest in property through a pension – it's essential to know whether the tax reliefs make it all worthwhile.

- Pension plans offer three major tax breaks: tax relief on contributions, tax-free investment growth and a tax-free lump sum when you start withdrawing benefits.

- Tax relief on contributions means you could end up receiving a 40% discount on your investments if you are a higher-rate taxpayer.

- When you contribute £100 to a personal pension the taxman will top this up and your total investment will be £128 (£100/0.78).

- If you're a higher-rate taxpayer you can claim a tax refund of 18% x £128 = £23.

- You can invest this extra money as you please.

- When you start withdrawing benefits from your pension you can take 25% as a tax-free lump sum.

- You are eventually forced to take 75% as a fully taxed compulsory annuity.

- It's essential when comparing different investment routes to have both investors investing in exactly the same income-producing assets. In our examples we assume that both investors put their money in annuities.

- There are two different types of annuity: compulsory and purchased. Compulsory annuities pay a higher income but are fully taxed. A lot of the income from a purchased annuity is tax free.

- In our examples we showed that a higher-rate taxpayer could earn 141% more retirement income than someone who invests outside a pension plan. Even after just five years the pension saver ends up with 65% more income.

- Basic-rate taxpayers also score heavily by investing through a pension. After five years you could end up with 22% more income and after 30 years you could be 48% better off.

- ISAs and pension plans both offer fantastic tax breaks. However, the pension route is by far the most attractive. Pension investors could earn as much as 52% more income than ISA investors. ISAs only allow you to invest a small amount each year and the future of this tax break is uncertain.

Chapter 4

Earn 57% More Income with a Commercial Property SIPP

Introduction

In his 1989 Budget speech, Nigel Lawson said: "I propose to make it easier for people in personal pension schemes to manage their own investments."

This resulted in the birth of the Self-Invested Personal Pension (SIPP). SIPPs have become immensely popular in recent years and there are now estimated to be around 100,000 people who use them.

The benefit of SIPPs over other personal pensions is simply greater *investment flexibility*. Compared with the sometimes small choice of investments from insurance company personal or stakeholder pensions, SIPPs let you create your own investment portfolio consisting of:

- Cash deposits
- Shares
- Government and corporate bonds
- Unit trusts and investment trusts
- **Commercial land and property**

Of course, it's the ability to invest in commercial property that makes them special to readers of this guide and the focus of this chapter will therefore be commercial property SIPPs.

At present you cannot put residential property into a SIPP but from April 2006 this all-important asset class will be on the menu. You can expect the number of SIPP products to explode when this happens. We'll be taking a much closer look at residential property pensions in the next couple of chapters.

In this chapter I'm going to look at all the ins and outs of commercial property SIPPs. I'll look at how you go about setting one up, how much they cost and, more importantly, whether they're a good investment or not.

You should read this chapter even if you're not interested in commercial property. A lot of property investors are wondering what shape residential property SIPPs will take when they're introduced in April 2006 but many of these questions can probably be answered by taking a close look at what's currently on offer from commercial property SIPP providers.

For example, a lot of investors are wondering how flexible the new residential property pension plans will be. It's important to stress that this has more to do with what the SIPP providers will allow and what sort of business they want to attract, than with the Government's own pension rules and regulations. A list of existing property SIPP providers' websites is contained below so you can take a look for yourself.

Why Invest in a Commercial Property SIPP?

The only benefit of investing in *any* pension plan is to save tax. In the last chapter we took a detailed look at the three tax reliefs available to pension savers. The same reliefs apply to all types of personal pension plans, including commercial property SIPPs, namely:

- Tax relief on contributions
- Tax-free investment growth
- 25% tax-free lump sum

Tax relief on contributions means someone buying commercial property can potentially get it at a 40% discount. Tax-free investment growth means all your rental income is completely tax free and when you sell the property you will pay no capital gains tax.

Although the tax reliefs are extremely attractive, you should not invest in a commercial property SIPP for tax reasons alone. In fact you should not invest in any asset for tax reasons alone. At Taxcafe we call this spending £1 to save 40p in tax!

What investors should always seek to do is *maximize after-tax returns*. This involves careful tax planning but, more importantly, investing in assets that generate solid growth. Let's face it, you'd rather pay 40% tax on £1,000 of profits than have no profits at all!

What this means to anyone interested in commercial property pensions is:

Only invest in a commercial property SIPP if you are going to invest in commercial property anyway. Investing in commercial property is a totally different ball game to investing in residential property.

That said, commercial property *is* an extremely attractive investment medium. In fact many property experts believe that, after a long period of fantastic growth from residential property, commercial property offers more potential over the next few years.

Direct Investment vs SIPP Investment

Since the only valid reason to invest in a commercial property SIPP is to save tax, it's worth pointing out that *direct*, non-SIPP, commercial property investment also offers a fantastic tax break.

Commercial property is generally classified as a 'business asset' for capital gains tax purposes. This mean it qualifies for business asset taper relief. In practice this means that 75% of your profits are completely tax free after just two years!

Compare that with residential property where the maximum taper relief is 40% and you have to wait 10 years to get it.

Because commercial property qualifies for business asset taper relief this means you can *never* pay more than 10% tax on your profits (40% tax on one quarter of your profits is equivalent to 10% tax on all your profits).

In practice, thanks to the annual capital gains tax exemption, you will probably pay much less than 10%.

It's important to stress that business asset taper relief, which exempts 75% of your capital gains, is not available if your property is let to a quoted company. So if you own retail property with a well-known high street tenant there's a good chance you won't get any business asset taper relief.

So exactly how valuable is business asset taper relief?

Example
Arthur and Jenny buy a commercial property for £150,000. Its value rises by 7% per year and after 10 years they sell it for £295,073. How much capital gains tax will they have to pay?

Three-quarters of their profits are completely tax free thanks to business asset taper relief. That leaves £36,268 taxable. However, they can also deduct their annual capital gains tax exemptions which will have probably risen to at least £11,200 each in 10 years' time. That leaves just £13,868 taxable.

If they manage to sell the property when their other income is quite low, Arthur and Jenny will only pay capital gains tax at the rate of 20%. This means their total tax bill would be just £5,547.

In summary, they've made a profit of £145,073 and only paid tax of £5,547. The total tax rate is just 4%, which is far lower than the 40% tax rate that most investors bandy about when they talk about capital gains tax.

You could argue that by investing through a SIPP Arthur and Jenny would have escaped tax altogether. This is a valid comment but the tax savings would probably all have disappeared in higher SIPP charges and it's important to bear in mind that they would have lost access to their money until they retired.

Why Commercial Property SIPPs Are Attractive

The above example shows that direct commercial property investors can largely escape capital gains tax. Does this mean commercial property SIPPs are a waste of time?

No, is the simple answer. Although capital gains tax is important, it's only one part of the equation. What the above example ignores is that a lot of commercial property investment returns come in the shape of *rental income*. Rental income is, of course, subject to income tax at rates as high as 40% if you invest outside a SIPP but is completely tax free if you invest inside a SIPP.

We've also ignored the most important SIPP tax break of all: tax relief on contributions.

Let's take a look at another example to see how these additional factors affect the overall picture. We're going to track two commercial property investors over 20 years and see who comes out on top: the SIPP investor or the direct investor.

To keep things simple we'll assume for now that *no borrowings* are used. We'll look at geared property investments later in the guide when we examine residential property SIPPs. For now we'll assume that the investors in the example buy a small share in a commercial property using their own money.

Example
Arthur buys a share in a small office development for £20,000. The rental yield is 5% and rents rise by 2.5% per year. The property grows in value by 5% per year. We'll assume he pays 40% tax on his rental profits and reinvests these in an ISA earning 5% per year tax free.

His friend Jonathan invests in an identical property through a commercial property SIPP. The only difference is Jonathan doesn't pay any income tax on his rental profits.

Jonathan makes a contribution of £20,000 into his SIPP. The taxman also makes a top-up payment (see Chapter 3) bringing

Jonathan's total investment to £25,641 (£20,000/0.78). Because he's a higher rate taxpayer he also gets a tax refund of £4,615 (£25,641 x 18%) which he invests in an ISA.

Who ends up better off after 20 years, Arthur or Jonathan?

Arthur – the Direct Investor

Arthur's share in the property grows in value by 5% per year until it is eventually worth £53,066. He now sells his stake in the office building and, thanks to business asset taper relief, the whole gain is completely tax free.

Turning to the income side, in the first year he received an after-tax rental income of £600:

£20,000 investment x 5% rental yield less 40% tax = £600

This income grows by 2.5% per year until, after 20 years, Arthur is earning £959 per year. He invests these profits in an ISA and after 20 years has built up a tax-free lump sum worth £24,352.

He now takes his total savings of £77,418 (£53,066 + £24,352) and uses them to buy a purchased annuity (see Chapter 3).

His total after-tax pension income will then be £5,102.

Jonathan – the Pension Investor

Jonathan's share in the property grows in value from £25,641 to £68,033 over the 20-year period. He pays no tax on his rental profits and after year one has £1,282 to reinvest:

£25,641 x 5% rental yield

This income grows by 2.5% per year until, after 20 years, Jonathan is earning rents of £2,050 per year. He re-invests these profits each year and, because they're held within a SIPP, no tax is payable. After 20 years, this investment will be worth £52,035.

When he made the pension contribution he also received a tax refund of £4,615 which he invested in an ISA. After 20 years this investment will be worth £11,633.

So in total Jonathan has got a share in a property worth £68,033, reinvested rental profits worth £52,035 and a tax-free ISA investment worth £11,633.

Jonathan now starts withdrawing benefits from his pension. He uses 75% of his pension savings to buy a fully taxed pension annuity. He withdraws the remaining 25% as a tax-free lump sum and uses this money and his ISA savings to buy a purchased annuity.

His total after-tax pension income will be £7,991.

Jonathan, the SIPP investor, ends up with 57% more income than Arthur the direct commercial property investor.

This is an interesting result. Arthur paid no capital gains tax at all when he sold his share in the property and we gave him the benefit of the doubt by letting him invest all his rental profits in a tax-free ISA (remember ISAs may not be around after 2010).

And yet despite all these concessions Jonathan the pension investor still ends up with 57% more income.

The reason Jonathan earns so much more is because he enjoyed tax relief on his initial investment and there was no tax paid on his annual rental profits.

Clearly commercial property SIPPs are an extremely powerful investment tool. In the following sections I'll take a look at some of the ins and outs: how to set one up, how much you can contribute, who are the main property SIPP providers and the pros and cons of geared SIPP investments.

Who Can Invest in a Property SIPP?

Not everyone can set up a commercial property SIPP. You can only contribute to one if you:

- are aged under 75.
- are resident and ordinarily resident in the UK.
- **do not belong to your employer's occupational pension scheme.**
- do belong to your employer's occupational scheme but have earned £30,000 or less in one of the last five tax years *and* are not a controlling director of the company. In this case you can contribute up to £3,600 per year.

I've highlighted the third point because it clearly is the most restrictive. If you are an employee you generally cannot invest in a SIPP. You can only make SIPP contributions if you do not belong to your employer's own pension fund or earn under £30,000 per year.

If this rules you out of investing in a SIPP don't worry – the law will be changing on April 6th 2006. Employees who already have other pension provision will then be able to contribute as much as they like to SIPPs as well. So it's worthwhile finding out a bit more about this fantastic retirement product even if you cannot invest in one right now.

At present SIPPs are aimed mainly at the self employed and those who do not belong to company pension schemes. Commercial property SIPPs are also extremely popular with owners of small companies who use them to purchase their company premises and claim a multitude of tax reliefs. More about this below.

SIPPs are particularly attractive to people who want to consolidate their various pension investments. For example, you may have changed jobs several times over your working life and accumulated benefits in a number of occupational pension schemes and personal pension schemes. You may have no idea how much these benefits are worth. By transferring these benefits to a SIPP you will be able to follow a more focused investment strategy... and invest in property at last!

Getting Money into Your SIPP

Let's say you want to buy a commercial property for £200,000. You cannot simply write a cheque for that amount and invest it in a SIPP. There are three ways to get cash into a SIPP:

- By making new contributions, or

- Transferring savings from other pension schemes, or

- By borrowing money.

Making New Contributions

How much you can invest in a SIPP each year depends on your age and income. The current contribution limits are as follows:

Age at 6th April	% of NREs	Maximum
35 or less	17.5	£18,480
36 – 45	20	£21,120
46 – 50	25	£26,400
51 – 55	30	£31,680
56 – 60	35	£36,960
61 – 74	40	£42,240

NRE stands for 'net relevant earnings', in other words income out of which contributions can be made.

Your net relevant earnings are usually your salary, bonus and benefits in kind if you are an employee or your business profits if you are a sole trader.

It does not include investment income such as interest, dividends and rents.

Tax Tip – Avoiding National Insurance

If you're a salary earner and pay pension contributions out of your own pocket you will be enjoying income tax relief but still paying a lot of national insurance.

What some smart employees are doing is stopping making personal contributions and getting their employers to make contributions for them.

To compensate the employer, the employee's salary is reduced by the amount of the contribution.

The end result is you won't have to pay any national insurance on this portion of your pay package – you've converted it from salary to pension contributions and pension contributions are not subject to national insurance.

Your employer, if he is understanding, can pay into your pension what he was paying you before *plus* the national insurance saving. He won't be any worse off and you'll be a lot better off.

Your employer's pension contributions are paid gross (before any tax is deducted) into your SIPP which is particularly attractive to higher-rate taxpayers.

Higher-rate taxpayers usually have to claim back higher-rate tax relief when they submit their tax returns. The time lapse between making your pension contribution and receiving the refund could be almost two years.

How much tax are you likely to save? It varies from person to person but, as a rule of thumb, you could save several hundred pounds per year in national insurance by following this strategy.

Example

George, aged 42, earns a salary of £50,000 and a bonus of £10,000. He does not belong to his employer's occupational pension fund. His maximum pension contribution in the current tax year is:

£60,000 x 20% = £12,000

There's also an 'earnings cap' of £105,600. So if George earned £150,000 per year he would only be able to contribute 20% of £105,600.

The current contribution limits are particularly restrictive to commercial property investors who wish to make large one-off contributions to their pension plans to pay the deposit on a property. For this reason investors in commercial property SIPPs usually make some initial contribution, transfer funds from other pension funds or buy just a small share of a building by investing in a commercial property syndicate.

Although the contribution limits are extremely restrictive right now, as we'll see in the next chapter, they will become a lot more generous from April 2006.

Transferring Savings from Existing Pensions

Another way of getting money into a property SIPP is to make transfers from your existing pension savings. If you've worked for more than one employer over the years there's a good chance you'll have accumulated pension rights in one or more occupational schemes. Most SIPP providers will let you transfer these rights, plus any savings you've accumulated in personal pension plans, to a commercial property SIPP.

This is one of the easiest ways of getting a large lump sum into your SIPP and giving your existing pension savings a new lease of life. Pension transfers are likely to become extremely popular in the next few years as more and more investors seek to give their pension savings a fresh start.

Note, you cannot take your existing pension savings as a cash lump sum. The money has to be transferred into another pension scheme.

There are several reasons you may wish to transfer from an old pension to a new SIPP:

- To consolidate all your pension savings under one roof.

- To benefit from wider investment choice, eg commercial or residential property.

- Because you don't trust your old occupational pension schemes to meet their promises, for example if the company goes bust and there is a pension deficit.

- Because you feel you can personally grow your pension savings better and achieve a higher pension than what you'd be entitled to from your existing pension arrangements. Some insurance company pension funds have delivered appalling investment returns in recent years, eg 3% per year over 10 years!

- To escape high charges from existing personal pension schemes.

- To enjoy benefits to which you may not currently be entitled, eg early retirement or income drawdown. (This reason is probably the least important because from April 6th 2006 *all* pensions will be governed by the same set of rules.)

The key is to ensure that the benefits you hope to enjoy are greater than the benefits you might lose from your old pension arrangements.

You also have to take account of any exit penalties and professional adviser fees or commissions for handling the transfer to your new pension.

It's important to stress that you *must* take professional advice and not rush into making a transfer. Seek out a financial adviser with what's known as a 'G60' qualification for handling pension transfers. You're probably better off with one who charges a fee rather than one who charges a commission. If the advice is on a commission basis the adviser will receive a percentage of the amount transferred but will not receive anything if a transfer is viewed as being inappropriate. This may sway the advice in favour of making a transfer.

Pension Transfers – How They Work

So should you or shouldn't you transfer your existing pension savings to a commercial or residential property SIPP? This is an extremely important question and one many people will be asking in the next few years. Here are some pointers to help you make up your mind.

- If you change jobs and leave your employer's pension scheme you can usually leave behind the pension benefits you've built up. Typically if you have been in an occupational pension scheme for a period of two years or more, you will qualify for a 'preserved' or 'deferred' pension.

- No more years of service build up but when you retire your pension is based on the final salary you earned, increased in line with inflation.

- If you decide you would now like to transfer to a new pension fund the benefits you've built up in your former employer's pension fund are converted into a cash lump sum known as the 'cash equivalent transfer value' (CETV).

- In an occupational pension scheme the CETV has to be calculated by an actuary. The CETV is simply the value *today* of the rights you've built up in the pension scheme. It's the amount of money you would have to invest today to get the benefits that would be provided if you kept your money in the pension scheme.

- When calculating the CETV, the pension scheme trustees will decide if they should take account of discretionary benefits such as pension increases – in most cases they don't. The cash value usually doesn't provide for lump sum death benefits, widows' pensions or dependants' pensions. So if you transfer you could lose some valuable discretionary benefits.

- If you wish to transfer from a final salary pension scheme a transfer value analysis must be carried out. This will allow you to compare the benefits of your frozen pension with what you hope to earn from, eg, a property SIPP.

  A 'critical yield' is calculated which shows how fast your new pension scheme will have to grow, eg 7 per cent per year, to match the benefits of your old pension.

- There may be stiff transfer charges if you transfer from a 'group' personal pension scheme in which you have a personal pension – check out with the plan provider.

- There are no surrender charges if you transfer from one of the new stakeholder schemes.

- If you have rights in an employer's pension fund that is in deficit, the pension transfer might reflect this as a percentage reduction.

- Investigate the financial health of your old scheme. If it is in surplus it may be worth leaving your funds invested.

- Don't transfer from your *current* employer's occupational pension into which both you and your employer are contributing. According to research from Brunel university, the average employer contributes 11% to final salary schemes and 5% to defined contribution schemes. By transferring you would lose this 'free money'.

- Don't transfer from public-sector pension schemes. These are the blue chips of pension schemes, offering full inflation protection and other benefits.

- Check out the death benefits of your former pension scheme which may not be matched by a personal pension scheme without having to buy a life insurance policy.

- Don't bother transferring if you have just a small amount of money in your former pension. It's arguably only worth transferring if you have more than £10,000 invested.

- It may be reckless and expensive to transfer if you are less than 10 years away from retirement.

- If you transfer from a final salary scheme to a SIPP you give up the promise of a fixed level of pension income and are now dependent on how well you can grow your money. You will also have to pay the costs of running the plan.

In summary, you may have a lot to gain by transferring savings from old pension plans to a new property SIPP, especially if you are many years away from retirement and believe you can grow your investments faster than most pension fund managers. Pension transfers are one of the easiest ways of getting money into a SIPP.

However, you also potentially have a lot to lose if your existing pension funds offer a variety of benefits that will be taken away and if the transfer charges are high.

Borrowing Money to Invest in SIPPs

The third and final way of getting money into a SIPP to fund the purchase of a commercial property is to borrow money. The current borrowing limit is 75% of the *purchase price* of the property. The remaining 25% has to come out of your own pocket.

You will be personally responsible for organizing a mortgage. Your SIPP provider will not do this for you, although it may have links with commercial lenders.

Commercial property mortgages are more difficult to obtain than residential property ones. They're usually more 'tailor made' and the terms (the interest rate charged and the length of the mortgage) are dependent on the quality of your tenant and the length of the lease.

The mortgage terms will also depend on what type of commercial property you wish to buy: industrial, retail or offices but loans of 75% are widely available for periods of up to 25 years. A typical interest rate would be the Bank of England base rate plus between 1.5% and 3%.

A good source of information on commercial property mortgages is: www.mortgagesforbusiness.co.uk

Possibly the least attractive of the reforms coming into play on April 6 2006 is the new borrowing rule for pension funds. From that day your borrowing will be limited to just 50% of your pension plan's *net assets*.

At present if you want to buy a commercial property for £100,000 you only have to personally contribute £25,000 (in other words, 25% of the purchase price). From April 6th 2006 you will need to put up £67,000, against which you can then borrow the remaining £33,000.

Because the pension borrowing limits are to be so severely curtailed, many commercial property investors are trying to invest as much as possible before A-Day.

Who Offers Commercial Property SIPPs?

The number of SIPP providers has exploded in recent years. However, not all offer commercial property SIPPs. Some that do include:

- Suffolk Life - www.suffolklife.co.uk
- James Hay - www.jameshay.co.uk
- Pointon York - www.sippsolutions.com

- Talbot and Muir - www.talbotmuir.co.uk
- AJ Bell - www.ajbell.co.uk
- Capita PPML - www.ppml.co.uk

You'll find a wealth of information about commercial property SIPPs on these websites.

If you're interested in starting a commercial property SIPP make sure you speak to your own IFA first. A good one will have had dealings with some of these firms and know which ones offer the best deal and standard of service.

How Much Do SIPPs Cost?

The main drawback of SIPPs is their fees. Because SIPPs are – to use that dreadful word – 'bespoke' investments, the costs are higher than for off-the-shelf investment products. There is a growing number of online SIPP providers with very low charges but these do not offer commercial property SIPPs.

You will have to pay both set-up fees and ongoing fees. Set-up fees include the SIPP administrator's fee and the same costs you incur when buying any property: legal fees, surveyor's fees, lender's fees etc. Ongoing fees include the SIPP administrator's charges, surveyor's fees, property management company fees and legal fees. All these fees will normally be paid out of your SIPP bank account and not from your own pocket.

You may also end up paying fees to your IFA.

To give you some idea of the actual costs, below in Table 10 are the fees of a well-known SIPP administrator. They're by no means meant to be representative but do serve as a good starting point.

Table 10
James Hay – SIPP Fees

Set-up Fees:
- Property transaction fee: £550 +0.1% over £400,000
- Solicitors: £850 for purchase up to £400,000 plus £300 if a new lease is required plus £300 where a mortgage is required

Ongoing Fees:
- Annual Property Administration Charge: £500 for each letting
- Annual Mortgage Administration Charge: £100

Buying Your Business Premises

Commercial property SIPPs have become extremely popular in recent years with company owners, who use them to buy their company's premises through their own pension plans. The advantages are the following:

- The company pays rent to the SIPP. This rent is a tax-deductible expense.

- The SIPP pays no income tax on the rental profits.

- When your pension fund sells property there is no capital gains tax.

- The property is owned by your pension fund. This will protect you if you or your company become insolvent.

- All legal and other costs can be paid out of your SIPP savings.

- The SIPP can reclaim VAT on property improvements.

- When you take your pension the income can be paid from rental income.

Example

Paul and Yasmin own a successful web design business. Instead of wasting money on rent they decide they would like to own their own business premises. They're delighted to discover that a commercial mortgage will not cost more than they are currently paying their landlord.

They decide to establish SIPPs to buy the property. Their existing pension savings were with an insurance company but, after taking professional advice, they decide to transfer the funds to a well-known commercial property SIPP provider.

The company will have to pay rent at the proper market rate to their SIPPs and this can be used to pay off the bank borrowings.

They will also be able to make regular annual contributions to reduce the mortgage. These contributions will, of course, attract tax relief.

The investment could be structured as follows:

Property Purchase Price	£150,000
Fees and Costs:	
Stamp Duty – 1%	£1,500
Legal fees	£1,000
Valuation	£500
SIPP provider fees	£500
	£3,500
Total Cost	**£153,500**

The investment could be paid for as follows:

Bank borrowing	£150,000 x 75%	£112,500
Pension transfers		£25,000
Pension contributions	£12,480/0.78	£16,000

Total Funding £153,500

Sales Between Connected Persons

It's important to point out that you cannot sell your existing company premises to your SIPP. Transactions between a SIPP and the SIPP holder, or anyone connected with them, are currently prohibited.

So in the above example, if Paul and Yasmin had already owned the building and wanted to transfer it into a SIPP this would not be possible. They would have to move to new premises.

However, from April 6th 2006 these onerous 'connected person' rules will be abolished – see Chapter 5. The new rules will allow anyone to sell property they already own to a SIPP.

What Kind of Commercial Property is Allowed?

Your SIPP provider will consider your property purchase and decide whether it meets the relevant criteria. To carry out this evaluation you will be asked to submit a 'property questionnaire', which will provide all the relevant details of the property.

However, examples of acceptable property include:

- Hotels
- Guest Houses
- Nursing Homes
- Shops
- Offices
- Warehouses

- Agricultural land
- Forestry
- Business Units

Property that is not acceptable includes:

- Holiday accommodation and caravan parks
- Property that is used for recreational or leisure purposes
- Any land adjacent to residential property owned by you

Commercial Property Syndicates

Very few private investors have pockets deep enough to buy a good quality commercial property themselves, even with a mortgage. As a result, joining a property SIPP syndicate is possibly a very attractive way of investing in commercial property.

There are two distinct advantages of investing through a syndicate:

- Access to high-quality commercial property, for example, properties valued at up to £5 million.

- Because the initial investment is relatively small (for example, £50,000) they allow you to spread your risk by investing in more than one commercial property.

Some SIPP providers such as Pointon York specialise in setting up property syndicates for SIPP investors.

The key factor determining the success of any syndication arrangement is how easy it is to *sell* your investment when you want out.

Just think about it; if you hold shares in a listed company you can sell them instantly without incurring any sort of penalty. With property syndicates there is not necessarily an active market in their shares so you cannot be sure someone will buy your stake and, if so, at what price. It is therefore essential that the syndication agreement spells this out very clearly.

Property syndicates and other ways of buying small parcels of property, including residential property, are likely to grow in popularity over the next few years. This is because, with pension borrowing limits being severely curtailed after April 6 2006, many investors will not be able to afford entire properties, even small buy-to-let flats, and will have to invest in some sort of pooled investment scheme.

How a Typical SIPP Works in Practice

To give you some idea how SIPPs are set up and run, and some of the rules and regulations, I've compiled the following beginner's guide to property SIPPs. Most of the information comes from the existing providers of commercial property pension plans.

Bullet points and diagrams are used to make the information easy to read and digest.

I suspect many of these rules will apply to residential property SIPPs when they're launched, so it may be worth becoming familiar with the ins and outs of these plans now:

- The first thing you have to do is set up your SIPP account with your chosen provider – this usually requires evidence of your earnings and completion of an application form.

- Next you submit details of the property in which you're interested by filling out a property questionnaire. The SIPP provider will have to decide if the property complies with Inland Revenue and other requirements.

- For example, property currently cannot be bought from you, your close relatives, partners or any company associated with you. The property has to be bought from an independent third party.

- Development land and agricultural land is allowed but overseas property is currently not allowed.

- Property should be freehold – leasehold is permitted provided the lease is very long.

- You cannot enter into a contract to purchase the property and then ask the SIPP administrator to complete the purchase. This may contravene Inland Revenue rules.

- A surveyor's report is arranged to determine the suitability of the property. The purchase price must be close to the open market value of the property – 10% either way is usually allowed. These fees are paid out of your SIPP account.

- Often, but not always, the SIPP provider's own solicitors will be used to carry out the purchase of the property.

- All legal fees, stamp duty and other set-up costs will also be paid out of your SIPP account. Each SIPP has its very own bank account so you can keep track of where the money's going. This makes them very transparent investment products.

- Any VAT payable on the purchase price can be reclaimed.

- You have to ensure that there is enough money to buy the property and cover all costs before the purchase will go ahead. Payment can come from new pension contributions, transfers from your existing pension funds and bank borrowings.

- You will have to arrange the borrowings yourself but the loan will be in the name of the pension trustees who will have to be satisfied that there is sufficient income to meet the loan repayments and other costs.

- The lender must be a proper commercial lender (in other words, not a member of your family or a friend).

Figure 2
A Typical SIPP Property Purchase

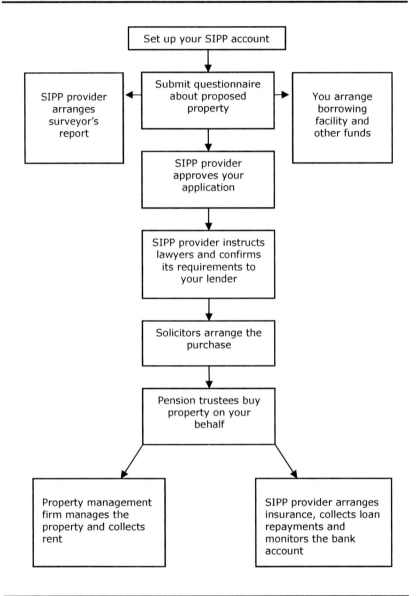

- You can borrow up to 75% of the purchase price or 75% of the development/refurbishment costs – no other lending is allowed. It's important to point out that many commercial lenders have lower allowable percentages, eg 70% of the purchase price.

- The loan will typically be on an interest and capital repayment basis.

- The lender has to accept that the SIPP administrator's liability for the loan is limited to just the sale value of the property. The lender must accept this term. The loan will also not be acceptable if it requires a guarantee from you, the SIPP holder.

- The rent on the property must typically be at least 110% to 115% of the mortgage payments if it is a fixed rate loan and higher if it is a variable rate loan.

- The pension trustees, typically an offshoot of the SIPP administrator, will be the legal owners of the property and the landlord, not you.

- A formal lease must be entered into at the time of completion unless there is already one in place.

- The lease must be for a minimum period, for example five years. It may have to be for a longer term if there is borrowing – the lender may require the lease to be as long as the mortgage period.

- The SIPP provider is usually responsible for managing the property and usually appoints a professional property management company to do this.

- To cover this, an annual property administration fee is paid out of your SIPP bank account.

- The SIPP administrator is usually responsible for making sure the building is properly insured because it is the legal owner.

- If your company occupies the property, the letting must be on commercial terms – you cannot overpay to get extra money into your SIPP or underpay to make life easy for your business.

- Development of a property can be undertaken from within a SIPP.

- Most SIPP providers allow a single property purchase by multiple SIPP members – a form of property syndicate. This can save on costs because there will be only one set of property purchase costs.

- Typically a central bank account is set up to receive the rents and pay the mortgage and surplus funds are then distributed to each SIPP member.

- It is possible to buy another member's share in the property and to do this a valuation is required.

- The partnership agreement should cover what happens on death, retirement and when new partners join.

Benefits and Drawbacks of Commercial Property

The critical question is whether commercial property is more attractive than residential property. In some respects it is. For example, most residential property leases are for 12 months or less. If you're lucky, your tenant will keep renewing for a few years but you could face an endless cycle of finding and negotiating with new tenants. While you do this your property could stand empty for at least one month in 12.

Figure 3
How a Typical Property SIPP Works

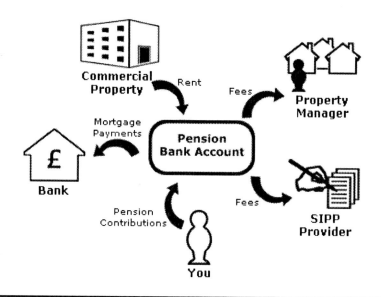

Commercial property leases, on the other hand, often last for five years or even longer with built-in annual increases. And if your tenant is a big financially sound company or, even better, a government organisation, you can simply sit back and watch the money come rolling in.

So commercial property can provide far greater income security than residential property and income security is extremely attractive if you have to make monthly mortgage payments or if you rely on the rents to pay your living expenses.

Commercial property tenants are also usually responsible for paying a host of expenses which are the landlord's responsibility in the case of residential property. Examples include maintenance and buildings insurance.

In other respects, however, commercial property is far less attractive than residential property. For example, it's generally much more expensive to buy and can be difficult to sell if you own specialist property.

Commercial Property Guide

If you would like more detailed information on how to invest in commercial property, the *Commercial Property Investment Guide* is available from our sister website

www.commercial-property.org.uk

It was written by Richard Bowser, the editor of *Property Investor News*, one of the country's leading property investment magazines and provides lots of relevant information and advice for budding commercial property investors.

Chapter 5

Generous New Rules for Pension Savers

There are many reasons traditional pensions are unpopular and shunned by people with money to invest. I listed these in Chapter 1 and they include lousy stock market returns in the early part of the decade and a string of reputation-crushing scandals.

However, the fact that existing pension products are unpopular doesn't mean property investors are unwilling to plan for retirement. I meet lots of investors at the numerous property shows I attend and one thing this diverse group of people have in common is their use of property to replace or, at the very least, supplement their existing pension arrangements.

This is backed up by academic research. For example, a study by the University of York has found that the majority of buy-to-let investors use property for pension planning purposes. They either buy property with the intention of living off the rental income when they retire, or they buy with the intention of accumulating retirement capital.

We already know from Chapter 3 that the tax reliefs available to pension investors are extremely generous and could add thousands to your retirement income. However, many property investors have been turned off investing in traditional pension plans because they associate them with *stock market* investing. Property is viewed as a much safer bet than shares.

Another factor that has put many investors off traditional pension plans is the extraordinary complexity. There are currently eight different sets of rules for pensions schemes dictating everything from how much you can contribute to where you can invest. This all makes life very difficult for the average investor and provides little motivation to save through these plans.

Others dislike the lack of flexibility when it comes time to retire and start taking benefits. At present, when you reach age 75 you have to buy one of those infamous 'compulsory annuities' (see Chapter 3) and when you die all your retirement savings arc generally wiped out. Many investors find this a serious turn-off.

Even if you do want to invest in a pension plan you might not be allowed to. As I explained in the previous chapter, if you currently belong to your employer's pension scheme you generally cannot make independent pension provision. This means you're stuck with what your employer thinks is best for you – in many cases it probably isn't.

The good news is all this is about to change.

April 6th 2006 is known as A-Day in the pensions industry because from that date there will be just one set of rules governing ALL types of pension plans. The new rules will give lots more flexibility to pension savers and provide new opportunities to many of those who have shunned existing products.

The Government is simply desperate to get us all to save more.

Most important of all for readers of this guide, the new pension regime provides some tremendous opportunities for long-term property investors. That's why this chapter is so crucial and why you should read it even if you currently don't have any regular personal pension savings.

Below I will hopefully translate these new rules into plain English and show you how to use them to your advantage. The new pension regime is not fixed in stone just yet but most of the details are known.

Why is it important to get to grips with these rules even though they haven't become law yet? Because the new pensions regime may have a fundamental effect on your retirement planning and investment decisions NOW.

You may want to take certain steps in the coming months or postpone others until the new rules are introduced.

Residential Property Pensions

At present you have a fair amount of flexibility when it comes to investing your pension savings, especially if you have a self-invested pension plan (SIPP). You can invest in unit trusts, individual shares, cash deposits and government bonds, in any mix you like.

And as we know from the previous chapter you can even invest in commercial property and many business owners have made the most of this rule by getting their pension funds to buy their company premises. This lets you pay rent from *your* company to *your* pension fund. The company can claim the rent as a tax deduction and the pension fund pays no tax on the income.

However, for many property investors this simply isn't good enough. The vast majority know very little about the specialist world of commercial property and many are unwilling to invest in something that they perceive as being almost as risky as investing in the stock market.

The good news is that, from April 6th 2006, residential property will also be on the menu. And the tax breaks that only commercial property investors can currently enjoy will be available to everybody.

Actually from April 2006 you'll be able to put your pension savings into virtually any assets including wine, art, stamps and even classic cars. Personally I'm not a great fan of collectables because I've seen too many people lose money on them. However, if that's your thing then A-Day will allow you to enjoy your hobby and save for retirement.

The inclusion of residential property in the list of approved investments is tremendous news for property investors and is likely to revolutionize the whole buy-to-let industry. In fact, you could say it's the most important development since the invention of the buy-to-let mortgage.

Allowing residential property will also revolutionize the traditional pensions industry. The insurance companies are no fools and are desperate to attract new business in what is a highly competitive market. Hence at least one major insurance company has started recruiting a large number of property experts so that it can start offering lots of exciting new products after A-Day.

Why are they so confident residential property pensions will prove popular? For the simple reason that property is the most popular type of investment and pension plans offer more tax breaks than any other. Put the two together and you have what can only be described as the most exciting investment opportunity in years.

As I showed in Chapter 3, these tax breaks can make an enormous difference to anyone wanting to secure a comfortable and happy retirement or acquire significant wealth and financial independence through property.

In certain scenarios you could end up with over 100% more income by investing inside a pension rather than outside a pension.

It's no easy feat making successful property investments. You have to make some extremely canny investment choices, juggle a variety of risks such as high mortgage borrowings and devote a fair proportion of your time to managing your portfolio.

Hence it would be a shame to ignore any tax reliefs that go begging. Many investors do just that and something like £1 billion in pension tax relief is wasted each year.

So what exactly are the tax incentives to invest in a residential property pension from April 6th 2006? In Chapter 3 I listed the three current pension tax reliefs:

- Tax relief on contributions
- Tax-free investment growth
- Tax-free lump sum when you retire

All three of these exist at present and will still be around after A-Day. However, the most important one, tax relief on contributions, will become much more generous and much more flexible.

Let's examine how each of these tax reliefs will benefit investors in residential property:

Tax Benefit #1
Tax Relief on Contributions

Being able to claim tax relief on your contributions to a residential property pension effectively means you can buy property at a 40% discount.

It sounds almost too good to be true and yet this fantastic state of affairs will exist from April 2006. Just imagine buying a property for £100,000 with the taxman stumping up £40,000 of the bill.

Building a property portfolio doesn't get much easier than that!

Tax relief on contributions is *the* most important tax break offered by pension plans and is likely to be the main driving force when it comes to setting up a residential property pension.

At present, however, the contribution limits are quite stingy. For example, members of occupational pension schemes can only contribute up to 15% of their earnings and members of personal pension schemes can only contribute between 17.5% and 40%, depending on their age.

Of course for most people these limits are more than adequate. Very few of us put away as much as 15% of our salaries, let alone 40%. However, there are times when being able to make large one-off pension contributions could be extremely powerful. I'll show you why below.

Another problem with the current system is that members of occupational pension schemes generally cannot contribute to any other type of pension.

This means many employees currently cannot set up their own commercial property SIPPs. You can only contribute to a personal pension if you have income from other sources, for example another job or profits from a small business.

There is actually one exception to this rule. If you earn £30,000 or less you can contribute £3,600 per year to a stakeholder pension. It's not a lot but it's a help.

However, for most employees the 'company pension only' rule places enormous restrictions on their retirement planning.

Generally you have no control over how your employer's pension fund invests your retirement savings. For example, if you're very young you may want to invest most of your pension savings in stock market investments or property rather than conservative bonds or other low-growth investments. Or if you're a knowledgeable property investor you may want to invest *all* of your retirement capital in property. No company pension scheme will let you do this.

You may not be forced to join your employer's pension scheme but foregoing this benefit could be crazy. Why? For starters your employer will probably be paying contributions out of his own pocket and these could be as much as 10% of your salary.

Occupational pension funds also offer other benefits such as free life insurance and disability insurance.

So many employees are currently in a difficult position – not wanting to lose their employer's pension benefits but also not entirely convinced their pension savings are being properly invested.

However, from April 6th 2006 the restrictive contribution limits and membership rules will be scrapped.

From A-Day you'll be able to contribute generally as much as you like to as many pension plans as you like and decide for yourself how your savings are invested.

You'll be able to enjoy all the benefits of belonging to your employer's pension scheme and contribute to a property pension plan at the same time.

From A-Day there will be just one contribution rule governing both occupational and personal pension schemes. The annual amount you can contribute will be drastically increased.

You'll be able to invest the *lower* of:

- Your entire annual earnings or
- £215,000

So if you earn, say, £60,000 in salary or business profits you'll be able to make pension contributions of £60,000 and effectively pay no income tax on your earnings.

The annual allowance will then be increased over time as follows:

- 2007 tax year - £225,000
- 2008 tax year - £235,000
- 2009 tax year - £245,000
- 2010 tax year - £255,000

Other important points to note about the new contribution limits are the following:

- 'Earnings' are not likely to include investment income (for example, rental income and dividends). In other words, if you're earning lots of rental income it will *not* be allowed as earnings when it comes to making pension contributions.

- Everyone will still be able to invest a minimum of £3,600 per year, as is the case now, even if you are not earning anything.

- If your contributions exceed the maximum allowed a charge of 40% will be levied. However, in practice most people will be able to invest as much as they like and enjoy full tax relief, without being bound by arbitrary contribution limits.

- Both an employer and employee's contributions count towards the annual allowance. In other words, the contributions of both you and your employer must not exceed £215,000.

- 'Carry back' rules which help you maximise your pension tax relief by making contributions in the current tax year but have them treated for tax purposes as if they were paid in the previous tax year will no longer be necessary and will therefore be scrapped.

The current methods of giving tax relief on personal contributions to pension schemes will continue:

- **Net Pay Method**. If you are making contributions to your employer's pension scheme, your employer only calculates PAYE after deducting your pension contributions. This gives you tax relief at your marginal rate of income tax and no further claim is necessary.

- **Relief at Source**. Your contributions are treated as having had an amount deducted equal to the basic rate of income tax. The pension scheme administrator claims this money from Inland Revenue and credits it to your pension plan. If you are a higher rate taxpayer you can claim higher rate relief via your tax return.

  In Chapter 3 I illustrated how tax relief is given to someone contributing to a pension scheme. For example, if the total contribution to your pension plan is £5,000, only 78% or £3,900 of that is paid by you. The remaining 22% is paid in by the taxman and represents your basic-rate tax relief. If you're a higher rate taxpayer a further £900 in higher-rate relief can be claimed when you submit your tax return.

Opportunities for Small Company Owners

If you own your own company you could benefit significantly from the new contribution rules. Pension contributions made by an employer company will NOT be restricted to the level of your 'earnings'.

In other words, if you earn a salary of just £10,000 your employer will be able to make a pension contribution of up to £215,000 and claim the whole amount as a tax deduction.

This is potentially a fantastic concession and should lead to some very creative tax planning by owners of small companies. Many companies might be able to completely avoid paying any corporation tax by paying generous pension contributions on behalf of their directors.

At present, shareholders/directors of small companies usually take a higher proportion of dividends than salary. This can save both the company and the owner/director thousands of pounds in income tax, corporation tax and national insurance.

However, while salaries are classified as 'earnings', dividends are not. So if most of your income comes in the shape of dividends neither you nor your company can currently contribute much to a personal pension.

However, from April 6th 2006 companies may be able to make large pension contributions regardless of the earnings of the director. These should be a tax-deductible expense for the company and, once invested, these contributions would be able to grow for the benefit of the member completely free of income tax and capital gains tax.

How Big Contributions Will Help Property Investors

While most people will continue contributing just a small percentage of their earnings to their pension schemes, the new

'100% of earnings' rule could be extremely helpful to those investing in property, which usually requires a lump sum investment of some description.

The new contribution rule will also be extremely attractive to those earning windfall profits, bonuses and other large but irregular lump sums. For the first time it will be possible to invest these amounts (which are usually taxed at 40%) in a pension plan and obtain full tax relief.

The new contribution limit will also be useful to property investors who are selling existing properties and reinvesting in a SIPP. These transactions will be subject to capital gains tax BUT the very act of contributing the money to a pension will reduce the rate of capital gains tax. This is because capital gains are taxed at your maximum marginal rate of tax (usually 40%) but pension contributions have the effect of extending the amount that is taxed at just 20%.

The examples that follow will show you how much tax relief those making large pension contributions are likely to enjoy. However, to understand how tax relief is given on big pension contributions it's worth briefly going back to basics and explaining how your income tax bill is calculated.

The basic income tax calculation goes like this: The first £4,895 of your earnings is completely tax free – this is your personal allowance. The next £2,090 is taxed at 10% (the starting rate), the next £30,310 is taxed at 22% (the basic rate) and all the rest is taxed at 40% (the higher rate). This is summarised in Table 11 below.

Table 11
Personal Tax Rates 2005/2006

First £4,895	0%
Next £2,090	10%
Next £30,310	22%
The Rest	40%

Example 1

Tom earns a salary of £60,000. His total tax bill is calculated as follows:

	£
Earnings	60,000
Less: personal allowance	4,895
Taxable income	55,105

Tax

£2,090 @ 10%	209
£30,310 @ 22%	6,668
£22,705 @ 40%	9,082
Total Tax Bill	**15,959**

Now let's say A-Day has come and gone and see how Tom could benefit from making a large one-off contribution to a property pension plan. To avoid confusion we'll assume tax rates stay the same in the 2006/2007 tax year as they are in the current 2005/2006 tax year.

Example 2

Let's say Tom has accumulated £39,000 in a savings account. He'd like to invest this money in a residential property pension. Because he has earnings of £60,000 he is allowed to make a 'gross contribution' of up to £60,000 and claim full tax relief against his earnings.

From Chapter 3 we know that Tom's 'gross contribution' will be £50,000 (£39,000/0.78) which is less than his earnings and therefore qualifies for full tax relief in terms of the new contribution limits.

Tom will personally invest £39,000 and the taxman will top this up with another £11,000 bringing his total contribution to £50,000. The £11,000 top-up payment is Tom's basic-rate tax relief and represents a repayment of some of the tax he has already paid on £50,000 of his earnings.

However, we know from Example 1 that Tom has also paid higher-rate tax at 40% on £22,705 of his earnings. He will already have received basic-rate tax relief on these earnings (22% of the 40%) when the taxman's pension fund top-up payment was made. However, he is still owed the remaining 18%. This will be refunded when Tom submits his tax return.

18% of £22,705 is £4,087 and this is the tax refund to which Tom is entitled.

For those who want a more technical explanation, higher-rate relief is given by extending Tom's basic-rate band so that income that would normally be taxed at 40% is now taxed at 22% - a saving of 18%. This can be illustrated as follows

	£
Earnings	60,000
Less: personal allowance	4,895
Taxable income	55,105

Tax

£2,090 @ 10%	209
£30,310 @ 22%	6,668
£22,705 @ 22%	4,995
Total Tax Bill	**11,872**

So Tom's tax bill has fallen from £15,959 to £11,872. Subtract one from the other and you get Tom's refund of £4,087.

In total Tom invests £39,000 and gets £15,087 in tax relief. This means he has £15,087 more to invest than someone who decides not to use a pension.

Example 3

Mandy, aged 32, runs a sole trader business selling second-hand clothes on Ebay. Her husband Colin makes enough money to support them both so most of Mandy's income is being used to build up a property investment portfolio. She has a terrific year and earns profits of £50,000. She wants to make a contribution of £40,000 to one of the new residential property pension plans.

Her personal contribution will be £31,200 and the taxman will make a top up payment of £8,800 bringing the total to £40,000.

Of her £50,000 profits, £12,705 is subject to higher-rate tax. So Mandy's higher-rate relief is 18% of this - £2,287.

In total she invests £31,200 and enjoys tax relief of £11,087.

Example 4

Ian and Kirsty inherit a house worth £200,000 from Ian's Aunt Betty. They decide that they would like to sell the property and use this money to build up a large property portfolio within a pension fund. They earn a salary of £40,000 each per year and are both members of their respective employers' occupational pension schemes.

As the law stands at present they would not be able to get any of Aunt Betty's bequest into a personal pension. Because they belong to a company pension scheme they can only contribute into their employer's scheme and the maximum total contribution is 15% of their salaries.

From April 6th 2006 they will have much more flexibility. They will be able to set up a property pension and make large lump sum contributions.

It may take Ian and Kirsty three or four *tax* years to get all the money into the pension fund while sticking to the annual contribution limits. But if they're fortunate with their timing, this could be done in a period of just over 12-24 months (eg one contribution on April 5th in the first year, one the next day on April 6th and then one on April 6th the next year).

So how much tax relief will Ian and Kirsty get as a result? To keep things simple let's illustrate this example using this year's tax rates and tax bands and pretend they stay fixed for the next few tax years.

Ian and Kirsty's normal tax calculation is as follows:

	Ian	**Kirsty**
	£	£
Salary	40,000	40,000
Less: personal allowance	4,895	4,895
Taxable income	35,105	35,105
Tax		
£2,090 @ 10%	209	209
£30,310 @ 22%	6,668	6,668
£2,705 @ 40%	1,082	1,082
Total Tax Bill	**7,959**	**7,959**

So their total tax bill is £15,918 which comes to a total of £63,672 over four years.

They've both got £100,000 to invest in their pension plans so let's say they do this over a period of four tax years. They each contribute £25,000 per year and the taxman tops this up by £7,051 each per year. Their total basic-rate tax relief comes to £56,410 after four years.

They're also each entitled to higher rate relief on £2,705 per year – the amount of their salary that is taxed at 40%. This comes to £487 each per year (£2,705 x 18%) – a total tax saving of £3,895 over four years.

Their total tax relief is £60,305. In other words they have £60,305 more to invest than someone who decides not to invest through a pension.

Example 5

Aru, aged 43, is a high-flying salesman and earns a salary of £40,000 and a bonus of roughly £40,000. He decides he'd like to invest his bonus in property. He doesn't belong to an occupational pension scheme.

His current tax calculation is as follows:

	£
Salary and bonus	80,000
Less: personal allowance	4,895
Taxable income	75,105

Tax

£2,090 @ 10%	209
£30,310 @ 22%	6,668
£42,705 @ 40%	17,082
Total Tax Bill	**23,959**

Under the current laws he could invest 20% of his salary and bonuses in a personal pension. His maximum gross contribution would be just £16,000. Under the new rules he can make a much larger lump sum contribution in years when he earns big bonuses.

Aru decides to make a personal contribution of £40,000. The taxman will make a top-up contribution of £11,282 bringing his total pension contribution to £51,282.

He's already paid higher rate tax on £42,705 of his earnings so he can claim back an extra £7,687 (£42,705 x 18%) when he submits his tax return.

In total Aru will enjoy tax relief of £18,969.

Maximizing Your Tax Relief

In all of the above examples the pension investors enjoyed significant tax relief on their lump sum pension contributions.

However, none of them enjoyed the highest tax relief possible. They all received full basic-rate tax relief (the 22% contributed by the taxman to the pension plan) but none of them received higher-rate tax relief on the *entire pension contribution* – despite the fact that they were all higher-rate taxpayers.

The reason none of the individuals in the examples received full higher-rate tax relief is that none of them had sufficient income taxed at 40%. Remember you only get higher-rate tax relief to the extent that you have earnings taxed at 40%.

So if only £5,000 of your earnings is taxed at 40% you will only receive higher-rate tax relief on £5,000... even if you make a £20,000 pension contribution.

Even though the new pension contribution limits allow you to make large one-off pension contributions this might not necessarily be the best thing to do, unless you have a lot of income taxed at 40%.

To enjoy the maximum tax relief – and ensure that you really are getting your investments at a 40% discount – it may pay to spread your contributions over a number of tax years. The idea here is to make contributions equivalent to the amount of your income that is taxed at 40%.

This strategy may not suit all investors, being more drawn out, but is the only way to ensure that you enjoy the maximum tax savings.

Summary

The new pension contribution rules are enormously attractive to most investors and savers for the following reasons:

- You will be able to belong to your employer's occupational pension scheme and contribute to a personal pension plan at the same time.

- You will be able to contribute an amount equal to your entire annual earnings and obtain tax relief. This is fantastic for property investors who have other resources at their disposal and want to invest a large lump sum.

- It's also good news for those like Aru in the above example who earn large bonuses or other windfall payments that are usually heavily taxed.

- To enjoy the highest possible tax relief you should, however, only contribute an amount equivalent to that part of your earnings that is taxed at 40%.

Tax Benefit #2
Tax-free Investment Returns

The other major benefit of investing in residential property through a pension is tax-free investment returns. For a property investor this means earning rental income that is completely tax free. So instead of paying up to 40% income tax on your rental profits you will pay absolutely nothing. This will leave many investors with significantly more money to save up and eventually acquire new property.

Of course, if you are using borrowed money to invest in property, you probably won't have significant rental profits, especially in the early years. Most of your rental income will go towards paying mortgage interest. However, as the years go by your rents are likely to grow producing a rental profit at some stage. This is where the pension tax relief will be very valuable.

And it's not just your rents that will escape tax when you invest via a pension fund. The tax most property investors dread is capital gains tax which, in the worst case scenario, can also eat up 40% of your profits.

However, it's worth pointing out that CGT is often not as onerous as most investors expect. Thanks to the many reliefs on offer you are likely to end up paying far less than the 40% rate that most investors bandy about, even if you are a higher-rate taxpayer.

Thanks to taper relief (which protects as much as 40% of residential property profits from the taxman) and the annual CGT exemption (which protects a further £8,500 per person), your 'effective tax rate' will usually be much lower than 40%.

By 'effective tax rate' we mean the total tax expressed as a percentage of your profits.

For example, Table 12 contains some effective tax rates of higher-rate taxpayers earning different amounts of profit over different time periods. The first block of tax rates is for married couples (who enjoy two CGT reliefs), the second is for unmarried investors. These figures are calculated after taking account of the annual CGT exemptions and non-business asset taper relief (the type of taper relief that residential property investors qualify for).

These numbers make fascinating reading because they show that, even if you are a higher-rate taxpayer, and earn tens of thousands of pounds in property profits, you may end up paying tax at a rate as low as zero to 25%, without resorting to any fancy tax planning.

Even if you earn profits of £200,000 you could end up paying no more than about 20% tax!

Remember these tables are for 40% taxpayers. If these investors were able to sell their property in years of low income or transfer a greater proportion to a low-income spouse the tax savings would be even greater. Some of the chargeable gain would then be taxed at just 20% or even 10%.

Although CGT rates aren't often as high as many people expect, being able to avoid this tax altogether is a distinct advantage of investing through a pension. For example, an unmarried investor who makes a £50,000 profit after five years will still have to pay over £13,000 in tax.

Table 12
EFFECTIVE CGT RATES

Married Couples

Profits	1 yr	3 yrs	5yrs	7yrs	10yrs
£10,000	0	0	0	0	0
£20,000	6	4	0	0	0
£30,000	17	15	11	7	1
£40,000	23	21	17	13	7
£50,000	26	24	20	16	10
£60,000	29	27	23	19	13
£70,000	30	28	24	20	14
£80,000	32	30	26	22	16
£90,000	32	30	26	22	16
£100,000	33	31	27	23	17
£120,000	34	32	28	24	18
£150,000	35	33	29	25	19
£200,000	37	35	31	27	21

Unmarried Investors

Profits	1 yr	3 yrs	5yrs	7yrs	10yrs
£10,000	6	4	0	0	0
£20,000	23	21	17	13	7
£30,000	29	27	23	19	13
£40,000	32	30	26	22	16
£50,000	33	31	27	23	17
£60,000	34	32	28	24	18
£70,000	35	33	29	25	19
£80,000	36	34	30	26	20
£90,000	36	34	30	26	20
£100,000	37	35	31	27	21
£120,000	37	35	31	27	21
£150,000	38	36	32	28	22
£200,000	38	36	32	28	22

Many investors are put off selling property that has risen in value considerably because they dread losing a significant portion of their profits to the taxman. The problem with this buy-and-hold strategy is you potentially miss out on investing in the latest 'hotspot' where profits are likely to be higher.

Investing through a pension could solve this problem. Because there is no capital gains tax to worry about, you will be able to sell and buy property more frequently and hopefully earn greater returns.

Tax-free Re-mortgaging

The fact that returns from property pensions are tax free provides an extra and little-known opportunity for property investors. Many grow their portfolios by re-mortgaging their existing properties. Unfortunately most don't understand the tax dangers of their actions.

For example, let's say you bought property A for £200,000 using a buy-to-let mortgage and five years later it's worth £300,000. You can release the £100,000 profit by re-mortgaging property A and using the funds to buy property B. Then in five years' time you could re-mortgage property A for another £100,000 to buy property C, and so on.

Refinancing existing property is a perfectly acceptable way of growing your portfolio. Because you're not selling any property there is no capital gains tax payable. However, you have to be careful when you do this. When you come to sell property A there may be a nasty capital gains tax surprise.

For example, let's say you eventually sell property A for £450,000 after 12 years. Just to recap, you bought the property for £200,000 using a buy-to-let mortgage and refinanced it twice for £100,000 and then sold it for £450,000.

After repaying the bank's original loan of £200,000 and the two lots of £100,000, you're left with a profit of £50,000.

But what about the capital gains tax bill? Remember the taxman completely ignores the borrowings on the property. All he's interested in is how much you paid for the property and how much you sold it for. The tax bill in this case, after deducting taper relief and the annual CGT exemption, could be as high as £57,000. In other words, the investor's tax bill is higher than his profits from the property and he'll have to dig into his pockets to find the extra cash.

This result comes as quite a surprise to many property investors, especially those re-mortgaging aggressively.

What about property pensions? Well, because there will be no tax on investment returns there will be no capital gains tax when you sell your properties. This could make re-mortgaging much easier and less risky.

However, what you will have to watch out for is the limits on pension fund borrowing. More about these in a moment.

Tax Benefit #3
Tax-free Lump Sum

This is the final major tax break enjoyed by pension savers. When you retire and start drawing your pension, 25% of your savings can be taken in cash as a tax-free lump sum.

This lump sum could be put to a number of good uses. You could use it to buy a rental property to boost your retirement income or to pay off existing mortgage debt on other buy-to-let properties that you hold personally.

(At present the cash lump sum received by members of company pension schemes is determined by length of service and final salary. After April 6th 2006 they too will qualify for a flat 25%.)

If you belong to a company pension scheme there's a good chance you are making Additional Voluntary Contributions (AVCs). At present you cannot take any cash lump sum based on your AVCs.

However, the good news is that from A-Day cash will be payable from all AVCs.

Property Pension Drawbacks

The advantages of property pensions are ALL on the tax front. What about the drawbacks? There are a few and some are more serious than others.

Drawback #1
Losing Control

The first major drawback is that you will not see your money again until you reach age 55. The new regulations will prevent you from getting your hands on any of your money until that date. (The current age is 50 but this will rise under the new pensions regime.)

What this means is that no matter what financial storms blow across your decks between now and the day you retire, your pension savings will not be there to bail you out.

For example, imagine a member of your family is seriously ill and needs specialist private medical treatment here or in another country. If all or most of your savings are in a pension plan you will not be able to get your hands on any of your savings.

Or what if you lose your job or your business gets into difficulty or you want to educate your children at expensive private schools or top universities. It's at times like these that you may regret locking a lot of your wealth away in a pension fund.

Personally I like to have a lot of control over my money. And I especially dislike it when Government bean-counters tell me what I can and cannot do.

However, it has to be conceded that it's those same bean-counters who also allow us to claim lots of tax relief on our pension contributions!

The question you have to ask yourself is, do the tax benefits outweigh the other drawbacks?

In Chapter 3 it was shown that by using a pension you could easily end up with between 50% and 100% more retirement income than someone who decides to invest outside a pension. Most investors would find those extra returns high enough to put up with the drawbacks.

Furthermore, losing control of your savings until you retire shouldn't be a problem if the reason you're investing in property in the first place is to provide a pension. And for most property investors this is the primary motivation.

Sure, it's a shame you cannot get your hands on any of your cash until you reach age 55 but the vast majority of investors probably don't need to withdraw their benefits any earlier.

Most importantly, losing access to your investments shouldn't matter if a property pension is just one part of your investment activities. What you have to remember is that this is not an all or nothing decision. The idea is not to put *all* your property investments into a pension, just some.

Drawback #2
Fully Taxed Pension

When you retire you can only take one quarter of your savings as a tax-free lump sum. The rest is usually used to buy what is known as a 'compulsory annuity' (see Chapter 3).

This annuity is fully taxed and you are taxed on both your interest AND your capital. So while there are tremendous tax benefits to investing in pension funds there is potentially a major tax penalty at the end.

However, it's important to note that those extra returns of between 50% and 100% that I mentioned above *take account of this final tax sting.* In other words, the upfront tax reliefs far outweigh the final tax penalty.

Furthermore, the new pension rules have some extremely good news in that pension savers will no longer be forced to buy a compulsory annuity. Instead we will all have more choice in structuring our retirement income payments. More about this later on.

Drawback #3
Borrowing Limits

Of course you wouldn't want to borrow money to invest in most assets such as shares or government bonds. However, with property it's different. It's usually difficult for most investors to buy a property of meaningful value without going to the bank.

At present, pension funds can borrow up to 75% of the *purchase price* of a property (commercial property in this case as only this type of property is allowed in a pension at present).

From April 2006 this borrowing limit will change. From then on your borrowings will be limited to just 50% of your pension plan's *net assets.*

By the way, it's not the reduction from 75% to 50% that should catch your eye, it's the replacement of the words 'purchase price of property' with 'net assets'.

The difference between the two phrases is massive. Some SIPP investors will be able to borrow more to invest in property but most will experience a dramatic fall in the amount of borrowing allowed and it may become difficult to invest in certain types of residential property unless you have significant pension savings already.

Example 1

Samantha has a pension plan with £200,000 of investments. It's April 2006 and she now wishes to buy a buy-to-let flat for £100,000 through her personal pension. Provided she can find a lender willing to provide the full amount, she will be able to use borrowed money to buy the whole flat as it is worth only 50% of her pension fund assets. In this case Samantha is better off under the new system as she hasn't had to fork out the 25% deposit currently required by commercial property SIPPs.

Example 2

Rob has a pension plan with £25,000 of investments. Under the current borrowing rules for pension funds he could buy a commercial property for £100,000 using £25,000 of his own money as a deposit and £75,000 from the bank. Under the new rules he will only be able to borrow £12,500 – 50% of his current pension fund assets. Rob is clearly much worse off under the new system.

It is clear that borrowing to invest in property will be massively restricted under the new pension rules.

This will be the most serious disadvantage of investing in a property pension.

In Chapter 1 I mentioned that one of the attractions of the 'buy-to-let model' is the ability to gear your investments and convert a return of 5% per year into a return of 15% per year. Clever use of gearing is one of the keys to acquiring significant property wealth.

Unfortunately, most pension investors will not be able to harness the 'magic of gearing' to the same extent that traditional non-pension investors can.

The stingy borrowing limits are also the reason why many property investors will rely on the generous contribution limits to get existing capital into their pension plans against which they can then borrow.

What Types of Property Will be Allowed?

Although the new rules may allow you to put *any* type of residential property into a SIPP, in practice your choices will probably be restricted by your SIPP provider.

How much investment choice you have will depend enormously on how competitive the market for residential property pensions becomes. The more competitive it is, the more choice you are likely to have.

As you will have gathered from the previous chapter, being a SIPP provider carries with it an enormous amount of responsibility to comply with regulations and buying a property through a SIPP is not necessarily straightforward.

Furthermore, many commercial property SIPP providers perform time-consuming property management tasks such as managing leases and maintaining properties. It's unlikely they will want to manage or be responsible for large portfolios of buy-to-let flats dotted around the country.

Because many SIPP providers will want to have close control over any properties on their books, you may find them buying blocks of flats and selling them to pension savers. This will not appeal to many property investors who like to have more control over where they invest.

Alternatively, there may be a large increase in the number of residential property syndicates. These are currently quite popular with commercial property investors because they let you buy a share in a large property development for a modest sum of money.

The advantage of property syndicates is they let you spread your risk by buying a small share of several property developments. And because the initial investments are quite modest it's often not necessary to borrow money to invest. Being able to invest a small lump sum in property may become quite popular given the tightening in the borrowing rules after A-Day.

Another way to buy residential property through a pension fund may be to invest in Real Estate Investment Trusts (REITs). This is a new type of 'unit trust for property investors' and is expected to be launched in the months ahead (for more information about REITs see Chapter 8). REITs will probably be listed on the stock exchange and pay most of their annual rental income out to investors. Their American cousins have delivered solid and stable investment returns over the years.

If this new type of property fund is launched it will probably represent the easiest way to invest in residential property through a pension. You'll be able to buy them in very small parcels, such as £100, and so they're ideally suited to a regular savings plan.

Weighing it All Up

From April 2006 it will be possible to put residential property into a personal pension plan. The critical question is whether this is preferable to holding property directly.

In the next chapter we will take a look at some detailed comparisons of personal versus pension ownership to help you make an informed choice.

However, the main pros and cons can be summarised as follows:

Property Pensions: The Benefits

- Tax relief on contributions, allowing you to buy property for what is effectively a 40% discount.
- Tax-free investment returns. Rental profits and capital gains when you sell property will be completely tax free.
- Risk-free re-mortgaging.
- Tax-free lump sum when you retire. 25% of your capital can be extracted tax free from the pension fund when you reach age 55.

Property Pensions: The Drawbacks

- Loss of control. When you start investing in a pension plan you will not be able to access those funds until you turn 55. For some this may be extremely inconvenient, for others it may be a blessing in disguise.
- Limited borrowing. At present most buy-to-let investors can borrow 80% to 85% of the purchase price of a property. If you open a residential property SIPP you will only be able to borrow 50% of the fund's net assets.
- Heavily taxed pension. When you retire and start taking benefits from your pension you are potentially taxed not just on your income but your capital as well.

Allowing property into pensions is the most exciting of the A-Day pension changes, however it's by no means the only one. Several other new rules are being introduced that will make pensions more flexible and powerful tax shelters.

In particular, the new contribution limit will allow investors to make large lump sum contributions which enjoy full tax relief.

There are several other important changes that you should also know about.

Other Important Pension Changes

Apart from the new rule allowing residential property into pensions there are some other important changes taking place on April 6th 2006. These include limits on how much you can save in a pension over your lifetime, a change to the age you can start withdrawing benefits, new rules that will allow you to sell property and other assets to your pension, and rules governing how pension income can be extracted.

I'll take a brief look at each in turn.

Lifetime Allowance

Funnily enough this is the change that has grabbed many of the headlines although it affects very few people at present.

The lifetime allowance will set a maximum for the amount of pension savings you are allowed to accumulate. The Government hates the idea that wealthy people can reduce their tax bills by investing in a pension fund. When the new rules come into force in April 2006 the cap will be £1.5 million. This will rise over time as follows:

- 2007 - £1.6 million
- 2008 - £1.65 million
- 2009 - £1.75 million
- 2010 - £1.8 million

What if your pension pot, either through hard saving or successful investment decisions exceeds the cap when you retire? In this case there will be a 25% tax charge on the surplus assets. You will also be allowed to take these extra funds as a cash lump sum. Doing so, however, will result in a 55% tax charge.

According to the Government, all existing pension rights under the old rules will be protected. Under the new rules no one will be penalised as far as their accrued rights up to April 5 2006 are concerned. In other words, all rights built up before April 6 2006 will be preserved. The new rules will apply to all pension savings made after April 6 2006.

Your pre-April 6 2006 pension rights can be protected in one of two ways:

- **Primary Protection**. If by April 5 2006 you have pension savings greater than £1.5 million you can use primary protection to avoid the lifetime allowance charge. You do this by registering the value of your pension fund with Inland Revenue by April 5 2009. This will then qualify you for your very own 'personal lifetime allowance'.

Example

Ian has a pension pot worth £3 million on A-Day, in other words double the £1.5 million statutory lifetime allowance. Ian registers his fund with Inland Revenue and is then always entitled to a personal lifetime allowance which is twice that of the statutory lifetime allowance.

- **Enhanced Protection**. Alternatively, anyone can register for 'enhanced protection' even if your pension savings are worth less than £1.5 million. It then doesn't matter how much pension savings you accumulate. No recovery tax will apply. However, you will have to stop making any new pension contributions.

Retirement Age

A new minimum retirement age will be introduced from April 2010. From that date 55 will be the minimum age at which you can start drawing benefits from a pension.

This rule will apply to both occupational and personal pension schemes.

For those with personal pensions this is a bit of a blow because the minimum retirement age is currently 50. However if you belong to an occupational pension scheme that has given you the right to retire at 50, you can still take retirement at this age.

When you hit the minimum retirement age you will be able to start receiving a pension without having to retire from your job. You will be able to withdraw from work gradually and combine work and retirement. This option is currently only available to members of personal pension schemes.

Small Pension Pots

This rule is likely to affect lots of people. At present if you have more than £2,500 invested in a pension fund you are obliged to buy an annuity when you retire.

After 2006 if you have a very small pension pot you'll be able to take most, if not all, of it in cash.

To be precise, if your savings do not exceed 1% of the lifetime allowance (£15,000 in 2006) the whole lot can be taken in cash and 25% of it will be tax free. The remainder will be added to your income and taxed.

For example, let's say you have pension savings of £10,000. You'll be able to take £2,500 as a tax-free lump sum and the remaining £7,500 will also be paid out after deducting 22% basic rate tax.

More than one policy can be cashed in this way, provided the total is less than 1% of the lifetime allowance.

Tax-free Lump Sums

From 2006, members of *any* pension fund will be able to take 25% of their pension savings as a tax-free cash lump sum up to a maximum of £375,000.

At present members of occupational schemes are limited to 3/80ths of their final earnings for each year of service. Personal pension plan members can already take 25% of the fund value.

If you've been making additional voluntary contributions (AVCs) there is currently no tax-free cash entitlement. However, the good news is that under the new rules, tax-free cash will be allowed from AVCs.

If you're entitled to a lump sum greater than 25% you can retain your right to the larger tax-free lump sum.

More Choice and Flexibility When You Retire

One of the major drawbacks of the current pension rules is the lack of flexibility when you start withdrawing benefits.

At present, once you reach the age of 75 you have to buy a compulsory annuity with all your pension savings after paying out any lump sum. This annuity will generally cease when you die.

Before age 75, members of some pension plans, such as SIPPs, can benefit from 'income drawdown'.

Income drawdown is extremely popular with wealthier pension savers who want to defer buying a traditional annuity and manage their wealth themselves.

Income drawdown lets you take your tax-free lump sum immediately and, instead of buying an annuity, only extract the investment income generated by your pension savings.

You do, however, have to take an annuity when you reach the age of 75. If you die before age 75, the surplus funds can be paid out to your beneficiaries less tax at 35%.

The fund does not fall into your estate and is therefore not liable to inheritance tax.

From A-Day there will be a lot more flexibility. The Government wants to keep the existing rules, which force you to use your pension savings to produce a pension income by age 75. However, you will not be forced to buy a traditional annuity. Instead you can pay yourself a new type of pension called Alternatively Secured Income (ASI).

A summary of the proposed income changes is contained in the pages that follow.

Income Before Age 75

Between the ages of 55 and 75 you will be able to use your pension savings to produce income in one of two ways:

1. Buy an Annuity.

Annuities were discussed in detail in Chapter 3. An annuity pays you an income guaranteed for life. Both the interest and capital portions are fully taxed.

Although annuities lack flexibility, the income from them is often far higher than from alternative investments. They will therefore continue to be popular with retirees who need to maximize their retirement income.

2. Use Income Drawdown – 'Unsecured Income'

Instead of buying an annuity you can simply draw money from your pension pot. A-Day will bring new opportunities for drawdown. There will be far more income flexibility. Any income you withdraw will be fully taxed and subject to the following rules:

- The minimum income in any year is £1.
- The maximum income you can take is 120% of the annual income which you'd get if your pension savings were used to buy an annuity.
- The maximum pension must be reviewed every five years.

This flexibility gives a lot of scope for constructive tax planning. Income drawdown is useful if you want to keep your pension savings invested for a few more years with a view to earning an even higher retirement income later on.

Example

Lee, after taking his tax-free lump sum on April 6ᵗʰ 2010 at age 60, has pension savings left of £350,000. He doesn't want to take an annuity just yet. Let's say using that £350,000 he would have been able to buy an annuity of £22,000 per year. Lee must therefore take a minimum of £1 income per year but no more than £26,400 (120% of £22,000). This calculation will have to be done again within five years, in other words before April 6ᵗʰ 2015.

Lee will be able to vary his income each year to suit his needs. For example, he may wish to take very little pension income during the year if he is selling investment property that he owns personally. If his other income is low this may allow him to pay capital gains tax at the 20% savings rate on some of his capital gains.

Income After Age 75

If you've been using income drawdown, when you reach 75 you again have one of two choices:

1. Buy an Annuity.

Same as above.

2. Take Alternatively Secured Income (ASI).

For the first time pension savers will not be forced to buy an annuity when they reach age 75. You will still have to keep three quarters of your savings locked away inside your pension plan. However, it will be possible to take a far more flexible type of pension called Alternatively Secured Income (ASI).

Despite its somewhat unappealing name, ASI is one of the most attractive of the A-Day changes and should convert many to pension investing.

ASI will be available to everyone, including members of company pension schemes.

The alternatively secured income rules will allow you to vary your income from year to year within the following limits:

- The minimum income you can take is still just £1.
- The maximum income you can take will be 70% of the maximum annuity that a 75-year-old could purchase.
- This maximum income has to be reviewed annually.
- You will be able to choose annually how much income you take within the minimum and maximum limits.

Being able to take alternatively secured income will be extremely attractive to wealthier investors who want to keep control over their pension savings instead of handing over the entire lot to buy an insurance company annuity.

The £1 minimum income rule means that, if you don't need to withdraw income when you reach age 75 (for example, if you have other savings and investments), you can keep reinvesting your property pension plan's rental income *tax free*.

The maximum income rule means that you can withdraw a reasonably high income without having to buy an annuity. For example, you could keep your pension savings invested in property and withdraw most if not all of your rental profits.

The maximum income you could withdraw would be 70% of the maximum annuity that a 75-year-old can purchase. This should still be sufficient income for many people.

For example, let's say a 75-year-old man with £100,000 can obtain an annuity of £9,600 per year (many insurance companies were quoting rates as high as this at the time of writing).

In terms of the new ASI rules he will be able to withdraw rental income of £6,720 per year (70% of £9,600) for every £100,000 of his pension savings. This translates to an income yield of 6.7%, which is probably more rental profit than most properties are able to generate. So the pension saver in this example won't have to worry about getting his hands on all his rental income.

This will be fully taxed just as it would be if he owned the property outside a pension.

Furthermore, taking ASI is not an all-or-nothing decision. At any time you can use your funds to buy a traditional annuity.

If you take ASI you will probably also be able to pass on pension savings to your heirs.

Leaving Money to Heirs

The death benefits under the new system are potentially attractive. For the first time pension fund members who live beyond 75 may be able to pass their pension savings on to their children and grandchildren.

I say 'may' because the A-Day pensions legislation is currently being tinkered with and the ability to pass on pension savings to heirs is one of the loopholes that may be closed.

If you do end up taking alternatively secured income, then on your death it may be possible to transfer the balance of your pension savings to another member of your pension scheme. So for your family to benefit they would have to be members of your pension scheme. This should be quite easy to arrange by setting up a 'family SIPP' to which all members of your family belong.

Initially it was thought that these transfers would escape inheritance tax. However, this is looking increasingly unlikely.

Nevertheless the new rules may still open the door for the first time to 'inter-generational retirement planning', with parents able to pass surplus retirement savings to their children and so on down the generations.

Even if inheritance tax is payable, this facility may still appeal to many pension savers. It would address one of the major criticisms people have with the current pension system that, when you die after drawing an annuity, your annuity savings revert to the life insurance company.

Selling Existing Property to Your Pension Fund

At present you cannot sell property you own to your pension plan. From April 6th 2006, however, you will be able to do this.

This change will be welcomed by many investors who want to transfer properties they currently own to a SIPP. For example, if you want your company premises to be held within a SIPP you currently have to move to brand new premises, with all the trauma this entails!

Residential property investors may also want to transfer existing properties to a SIPP rather than buy new ones. Of course, the crucial question is whether the costs of doing this outweigh the benefits. Selling property to a SIPP will generate a capital gains tax bill so you will have to weigh up your expected gains (pension tax reliefs) against all the costs (a capital gains tax bill, selling fees, stamp duty etc).

We'll look at this issue a bit more in Chapter 7 where we look at steps investors should be taking now before the new laws come into operation.

Your Home and Holiday Homes

Various newspapers and magazines have devoted many column inches to the story that from A-Day it will be possible to put your main residence or even a holiday home into a SIPP.

Personally I find the whole issue rather unexciting and hence the decision to give it just a small amount of coverage in these pages. Not only are the tax savings potentially very low, it will be technically impossible for most people to do.

The problem is that homes and private residences usually cost a lot more than buy-to-let flats or shares in property investment syndicates.

For example, let's say you don't already own your own home and want to get your SIPP to buy one. Let's say the property you want costs just £250,000 (I suspect many people reading this guide will have homes worth far more than this).

To buy this property you will need to have accumulated pension savings of £166,667 against which you can borrow a further £83,333 (50% of the pension fund's net assets).

Very few pension savers have this much money in their SIPP accounts or sufficiently high earnings to build up a pension pot of this size in a short space of time. Furthermore, very few homeowners can afford to buy a home with 67% coming from their own savings.

Alternatively, let's say you currently own your own home but want your SIPP to own it from now on. You will then have two options.

- **Sell the house and invest the proceeds in your SIPP.** Let's say the house is worth £200,000 and you have no mortgage. To get that money into a SIPP you will need to have earnings of £200,000 on which to base your pension contribution. If your earnings are *lower* you will have to spend several tax years getting the money into your SIPP account.

  If the house is worth more than £215,000 it will also take several years to get enough money into your pension plan regardless of your earnings because the maximum pension contribution you can make in any one tax year is £215,000.

  If you have a mortgage you have a further problem. Let's say you currently have a house worth £250,000 and a mortgage of £125,000. If you sell the house you will have net proceeds of £125,000 which can be invested in a SIPP (provided you have earnings of £125,000). The problem then is that you will only be able to borrow a further £62,500 (50% of net assets) and will therefore only be able to buy a home worth £187,500.

- **Sell your house direct to the SIPP.** If you like your existing home and want to keep it (as most people surely do), you could sell the property *direct* to your SIPP. The problem for most people will be finding the necessary funds for the SIPP to pay for the property. Because the property hasn't been sold, the owner will have to find sufficient spare cash to contribute to the SIPP in order for the purchase to go ahead.

  If a mortgage is involved this will further complicate matters. As we saw above, the bigger the existing mortgage the more difficult it will be for the SIPP to buy the same property while sticking to the '50% of net assets' borrowing restriction.

Even if you can overcome the above obstacles, having what is probably your most important asset locked away inside a pension fund, where you cannot access any of the capital until you retire, will place serious restrictions on your economic life.

Furthermore, the tax savings are potentially so small as to make the whole exercise farcical:

- For starters, your home is already completely exempt from capital gains tax so the only tax relief will be on your initial contributions.

- Putting foreign holiday homes in a SIPP will help you escape UK capital gains tax but will not help you escape any foreign capital gains tax.

- Private use of property will create a tax charge just as a tax charge is levied if you receive benefits in kind from your employer. This will be handled by incorporating a new section on your tax return where you'll have to declare any benefits-in-kind you receive.

- The much hoped for inheritance tax savings will probably not transpire because legislation may be introduced introducing a specific IHT charge to cover this loophole.

Summary

Apart from offering tremendous tax benefits such as tax relief on contributions and tax-free investment returns, pension plans will become much more flexible from April 2006:

- You will be able to belong to both your employer's pension fund and a personal pension plan.

- You will be able to invest in residential property inside a pension for the first time.

- You will be able to make large tax-favoured pension contributions which vary considerably from year to year and make it easy for you to get bonuses, inheritances and other windfalls into a tax-sheltered investment plan.

- You will be able to carry on working and draw benefits from your company's pension scheme.

- Before you reach the age of 75 you can draw a high income from your investment and keep control over your wealth. If you die, your heirs will receive what's left as a cash lump sum.

- After you reach the age of 75 you can still defer buying an annuity and take alternatively secured income instead. Although this is less generous it may appeal to wealthier savers who want to exercise control over their wealth and possibly leave a pension pot for their children.

Chapter 6

Earn 87% More Income with a Residential Property Pension

In the last few chapters we've learned a great deal about how valuable the pension tax reliefs are and how changes to all the other rules and regulations will make pensions more lucrative and flexible than ever before.

In this chapter it's time to answer some important questions: Will it be worth investing in residential property through a pension? Exactly how much more income are you likely to earn if you do?

The answers to these questions could have a profound effect on how you invest in property in the coming years. If pension returns are much higher than conventional property returns, you may have to rethink your whole investment strategy.

To help answer the 'pension vs direct property' question, I'm going to examine the progress of two different investors over a period of 10 to 30 years.

First of all meet Aaron, the IT consultant. He thinks pensions are dead boring and only for old codgers. He hates the idea of locking away his property investments for many years, even if there are some great tax benefits. He decides to give a pension a miss and invest in property directly.

Now meet Gordon, who owns a successful engineering business. He also isn't all that keen on locking his money away for many years. However, he does want to maximize his returns and retire with the highest income possible. So he decides to invest through a residential property SIPP.

We'll compare Aaron and Gordon's investment returns in three different scenarios:

- **Scenario 1**. They both invest in one residential property without using any borrowings.

- **Scenario 2**. They both invest in one residential property using borrowed money.

- **Scenario 3**. They both invest in residential property by making annual investments in property syndicates.

I'm not going to tell you how old Aaron and Gordon are because I've structured these case studies so they apply to *many age groups.*

The only assumption I'm going to make about age is that both Aaron are Gordon are 65 when they decide to retire. We'll then see how their investments have performed over periods ranging from 10 to 30 years. So if you, the reader, are 35 years of age now, you should focus on the long-term results. And if you're 55, take a look at how Aaron and Gordon do over 10 years.

What we're ultimately trying to discover is how much retirement income each ends up with. I'll make the same assumptions as in previous chapters: each earns modest investment returns, rental profits are reinvested, and so on.

Residential Property – No Borrowing

A-Day has come and gone and Aaron and Gordon each have £100,000 to invest in property (they may have, for example, inherited the money, earned large bonuses or business profits or sold other property investments).

Let's say they both manage to buy property that produces capital growth of 7% per year and produces an initial rental yield, after deducting all expenses, of 7%. I'll also assume that rents grow by 3% per year. Both Aaron and Gordon are higher-rate taxpayers earning £60,000 per year. This means Aaron's rental profits are taxed at 40% but Gordon's will be completely tax free because they're sheltered in a pension fund. Gordon's tax status will, however, affect the amount of tax relief he gets when he initially invests his money in the pension plan.

To be generous to Aaron, the direct investor, I'll assume that he reinvests his after-tax rental profits in an ISA each year and this investment produces tax-free returns of 7% per year. Gordon's rental profits are, of course, automatically reinvested tax free in his pension plan. Let's see how each investor fares over the years.

Aaron – Investing Outside a Pension

Aaron's progress is summarised in Table 13. At the end of year one Aaron's property has risen in value by 7% and is worth £107,000 and so it keeps growing until after 10 years it is worth £196,715, after 20 years it is worth £386,968 and after 30 years it is worth an impressive £761,226.

And what about Aaron's rental income? Remember he doesn't have any borrowings so his rental profits are quite high. In year one he earns rental profits of £4,200:

$$£100,000 \text{ x } 7\% \text{ less } 40\% \text{ tax} = £4,200$$

This rental income grows by 3% per year and you can watch the rents growing steadily in the third column of Table 13. Aaron prudently re-invests his rental profits each year in an ISA and earns 7% per year tax free. At the end of year one he has just invested his first year's rents which is why you see £4,200 again in the fourth column of Table 13.

At the end of year two he has new rental profits of £4,326 to invest in the ISA. What's more his original ISA investment has risen in value by 7% from £4,200 to £4,494. Taken together, his total ISA investment is now worth £8,820. And so it continues to grow.

Let's say Aaron decides to sell the property after a number of years (maybe 10 years, maybe 20 years, or maybe 30 years) and use his money to generate a secure retirement income. He's not earning a huge amount of rental income and feels he could do much better putting his money elsewhere.

Table 13
Aaron – Outside a Pension, No Borrowings

End of Year	Property Value	Rental Profits	ISA Investment
1	107,000	4,200	4,200
2	114,490	4,326	8,820
3	122,504	4,456	13,893
4	131,080	4,589	19,455
5	140,255	4,727	25,544
6	150,073	4,869	32,201
7	160,578	5,015	39,470
8	171,819	5,165	47,399
9	183,846	5,320	56,037
10	196,715	5,480	65,440
11	210,485	5,644	75,665
12	225,219	5,814	86,775
13	240,985	5,988	98,838
14	257,853	6,168	111,924
15	275,903	6,353	126,112
16	295,216	6,543	141,483
17	315,882	6,740	158,127
18	337,993	6,942	176,137
19	361,653	7,150	195,617
20	386,968	7,365	216,675
21	414,056	7,586	239,428
22	443,040	7,813	264,001
23	474,053	8,048	290,529
24	507,237	8,289	319,155
25	542,743	8,538	350,034
26	580,735	8,794	383,330
27	621,387	9,058	419,221
28	664,884	9,329	457,896
29	711,426	9,609	499,558
30	761,226	9,898	544,424

Before calculating how much income he can get let's see how Gordon's pension investments have performed over the years.

Gordon – Investing Inside a Pension

The important point to make about Gordon is that he first has to get his money into his tax-sheltered pension plan. He cannot just write a cheque for £100,000 and invest the lot in one go – he has to comply with the new '100% of earnings' contribution limit. His earnings are £60,000 per year so I'll assume he has made contributions of £33,333 per year over the last three tax years, which is well within 100% of his earnings and therefore qualifies for full tax relief.

(Note, although it takes Gordon three tax years to get his money into the pension plan he could theoretically do this in the space of just 12 months: by making one contribution at the end of the tax year on April 5th, one contribution the next day at the start of the new tax year, and the final contribution a year later on April 6th.)

Gordon has personally invested £100,000 but we know from Chapter 3 that the taxman will now top this up with a further £28,205 in free cash (remember the 'gross pension contribution' is calculated by dividing £100,000 by 0.78 which comes to £128,205). This means Gordon has an immediate head start over Aaron because he has almost 30% more money to invest in residential property.

Gordon also qualifies for higher-rate tax relief. I'll assume tax rates are the same as they are for the current 2005/06 tax year to keep matters simple. Just as in Chapter 5 his income tax calculation is performed as follows:

	£
Earnings	60,000
Less: personal allowance	4,895
Taxable income	55,105
Tax:	
£2,090 @ 10%	209
£30,310 @ 22%	6,668
£22,705 @ 40%	**9,082**
Total Tax Bill	15,959

Of his total income only £22,705 is subject to tax at 40% so this is the amount on which extra tax relief can be claimed. He has already received 22% from the taxman so the remaining 18% is claimed through his tax return:

$$£22,705 \times 18\% = £4,087 \text{ per year}$$

After making three pension fund contributions he will have received tax refunds totalling £12,261. We assume he invests this money in an ISA earning 7% per year.

Gordon's progress is summarised in Table 14. In column two we see his property, which originally cost £128,205, growing in value year after year. At the end of year one it has risen by 7% and is worth £137,179, and so on.

And what about Gordon's rental income? Like Aaron, he doesn't have any borrowings so his rental profits are quite high. In year one he earns rental profits of £8,974:

$$£128,205 \times 7\% = £8,974$$

You can see this number at the top of column three. This rental income then grows steadily by 3% per year. Straight away in year one Gordon is earning more than twice as much income as Aaron. Using the top-up payment from the taxman he has managed to buy a bigger property which delivers a higher rental income. Furthermore, he has not had to pay one penny of tax on his rental income.

His rental profits, when reinvested earn 7% per year, again totally tax free. At the end of year one he has £8,974 to reinvest, which is why you see that figure again at the top of the fourth column in Table 14.

At the end of year two he has new rental profits of £9,244 to reinvest. What's more, his original £8,974 has risen in value by 7% and is now worth £9,602. Taken together the total value of his reinvested rents is £18,846. And the investment continues to grow in this way year after year.

Finally, Gordon received pension contribution tax refunds of £12,261 which he reinvests in an ISA earning 7% per year. The progress of this investment is tracked in column five of Table 14.

Who Ends Up Better Off?

It's time now to tally up how each investor has done. Will Aaron, who thinks pensions are a waste of time, rue his decision to give up all those wonderful tax reliefs? I suspect he will.

We can see from comparing Table 13 with Table 14 that Gordon has significantly higher savings than Aaron (£2.2 million compared with £1.3 million) but what happens when both investors start using their savings to produce income. How much more income will Gordon earn?

This is the only number that really matters because the only reason to invest in a pension, or any investment for that matter, is to ultimately produce income.

Once again, to make sure we're comparing apples with apples, it's essential to assume that both investors put their money into income-producing investments that are as near as possible identical.

Table 14
Gordon – Inside a Pension, No Borrowings

End Year	Property Value	Rental Profits	Rents Reinvested	Tax Relief Reinvested
1	137,179	8,974	8,974	13,119
2	146,782	9,244	18,846	14,038
3	157,057	9,521	29,686	15,020
4	168,051	9,807	41,571	16,072
5	179,814	10,101	54,582	17,197
6	192,401	10,404	68,806	18,400
7	205,869	10,716	84,338	19,688
8	220,280	11,037	101,279	21,067
9	235,700	11,368	119,737	22,541
10	252,199	11,710	139,828	24,119
11	269,853	12,061	161,677	25,808
12	288,743	12,423	185,417	27,614
13	308,954	12,795	211,192	29,547
14	330,581	13,179	239,154	31,615
15	353,722	13,575	269,470	33,828
16	378,483	13,982	302,314	36,196
17	404,976	14,401	337,877	38,730
18	433,325	14,833	376,362	41,441
19	463,657	15,278	417,986	44,342
20	496,113	15,737	462,981	47,446
21	530,841	16,209	511,599	50,767
22	568,000	16,695	564,105	54,321
23	607,760	17,196	620,789	58,124
24	650,303	17,712	681,955	62,192
25	695,825	18,243	747,935	66,546
26	744,532	18,790	819,081	71,204
27	796,650	19,354	895,771	76,188
28	852,415	19,935	978,409	81,521
29	912,084	20,533	1,067,431	87,228
30	975,930	21,149	1,163,300	93,334

Therefore, I'll assume that Gordon and Aaron take their savings and do the following:

- Gordon uses 75% of his pension savings to buy a pension annuity for life.
- Gordon uses his 25% tax-free lump sum plus his ISA savings to buy a purchased annuity for life.
- Aaron uses all the proceeds from selling his property and his ISA savings to buy a purchased annuity for life.

Table 15 looks at the position after 30 years and shows how their income is calculated. I'll look at shorter time periods afterwards.

Gordon's total pension savings consist of the proceeds from selling his property – £975,930 – plus all his reinvested rental profits – £1,163,300 – plus ISA savings of £93,334. The annuity income is calculated using the same rates as in Table 3 in Chapter 3.

Aaron's total savings in Table 15 are shown as £1,168,670. This is the sum of his reinvested rental profits – £544,424 – plus the proceeds from selling the property for £761,226 and paying capital gains tax of £136,980.

Aaron and Gordon's tax bills are being calculated 30 years into the future and, of course, we have no idea what the levels of income tax and capital gains tax will be by then. However, to make the example as realistic as possible the current 2005/2006 tax bands and allowances have been adjusted for inflation, just like the Treasury does each year.

So how do their final retirement incomes compare?

At the end of the day Gordon ends up with income of £124,747 compared with Aaron's £77,017.

Put another away, Gordon's pension income is 62% higher than Aaron's.

Table 15 – Final Pension Incomes Compared

Gordon's Income Calculation After 30 Years

Pension Annuity:

	£
Total pension savings	2,139,230
75% Pension Annuity Purchase	1,604,422
Annual Annuity @ £7,280.4 per £100,000	116,802

Purchased Annuity

25% of £2,139,230 plus £93,334 ISA	628,141
Annual Annuity @ £6,819.96 per £100,000	42,839
Of which:	
Tax-free capital portion	35,622
Taxable interest portion	7,217

Summary

Total taxable income: £116,802 + £7,217	124,019
Less tax:	
@ 20%	14,714
@ 40%	20,179
After-tax income	89,126
Total capital income	35,622
Total Pension Income	**124,747**

Aaron's Income Calculation After 30 Years

Purchased Annuity

Total savings	1,168,670
Annual Annuity @ £6,819.96 per £100,000	79,703
Of which:	
Tax-free capital portion	66,275
Taxable interest portion	13,428
Less tax:	
@ 20%	2,686
Total Purchased Annuity Income	**77,017**

130

And what if we change some of the assumptions? For example, we were quite generous to let Aaron reinvest all his rental profits tax free in an ISA. The long-term future of this tax break is very much in doubt and it may gradually be phased out to encourage people to save through pension plans. If we assume Aaron pays tax on all his rental profits the gap between the two widens considerably.

Gordon, the pension investor, will now earn 87% more income than Aaron.

These results are quite amazing and show how powerful a tax shelter the new residential property SIPPS could be. Remember Gordon and Aaron started with exactly the same amount of money – £100,000 – and each earned *identical pre-tax returns*.

The only difference is Gordon put his money in a pension plan while Aaron invested outside a pension.

If that doesn't make you sit up and look twice at property pensions I don't know what will!

Shorter Savings Periods

The above example showed final income after 30 years which is equivalent to starting investing at the age of 35. Table 16 shows the final retirement incomes of Gordon, the pension plan saver, and Aaron, the non-pension saver, over shorter time periods.

I'm assuming that Aaron and Gordon reach age 65 after either 10, 20 or 30 years.

Income is calculated in exactly the same way as in Table 15 above.

The results speak for themselves. Even over short time periods Gordon, the pension property investor, still ends up with a lot more income than Aaron.

Table 16
Retirement Income over Different Time Periods

	No Pension	Pension	% Difference
After 10 years	16,587	25,172	52
After 20 years	36,346	60,637	67
After 30 years	77,017	124,747	62

Residential Property – Borrowing

The facts are exactly the same as before except this time we'll assume that Aaron and Gordon gear up their property investments by borrowing money.

In terms of the new borrowing limits for self-invested personal pensions (see Chapter 5) Gordon will only be able to borrow up to 50% of his pension fund's assets. Aaron does not face this restriction but to ensure that we are comparing apples with apples we will assume that he also borrows an extra 50%. I'll assume that they both pay interest on their mortgages at the rate of 6% per year.

Being able to borrow money means Aaron will be able to buy a property for £150,000 (£100,000 + £50,000 borrowings), whereas Gordon will be able to buy a property for £192,308 (£128,205 + £64,103 in borrowings). Remember Gordon has more money to invest thanks to the tax relief he has received.

Just as before they reinvest their rental profits tax free. However this time we also have to subtract their interest charges before calculating their rental profits. Furthermore, when they sell their properties we have to subtract their borrowings before calculating their final property profits.

So as not to bore the reader with endless examples, I'll just compare their final incomes after 20 years – a typical length of time to invest in a pension fund.

Aaron who invests outside a pension fund eventually sells his property, pays off his mortgage, cashes in his ISA and uses his capital to buy a purchased annuity. He will end up with an after-tax income of £45,809 per year. Compare that with the income of £36,346 he earned in the example where no borrowings were used (see Table 16).

This shows how borrowing money – or 'gearing up' your investments – can have a significant effect on your eventual returns.

And what about Gordon the pension investor? He eventually ends up with an income of £73,180 compared with the income of £60,637 he earned in the example where no borrowings were used. Once again clever use of borrowed money has provided a significant boost to the investor's final income.

It's not possible to borrow to invest in other assets such as shares which is one of the reasons why the new rules allowing residential property into pensions will be so popular.

Not only is Gordon much better off borrowing money to boost his pension savings, he is also doing much better than Aaron, who decided to invest outside a pension.

Gordon's income is 60% higher than Aaron's. Again, using the pension route has delivered handsome rewards.

Residential Property – Investing in Syndicates

In this example Aaron and Gordon make small annual investments in property syndicates, starting with £5,000 and rising by 3% per year.

This example is possibly very relevant because it is likely that many residential property SIPP investors will invest through syndicates rather than buy property directly.

Syndicate-type investments are particularly attractive because they allow you to spread your risk over a wide selection of properties in different geographic locations.

They also do not necessarily require you to make large lump-sum investments.

Fortunately for Gordon he will enjoy both basic-rate and higher rate tax relief on every contribution he makes to his pension plan. For example in year one he will invest £5,000 and receive a top-up payment of £1,410 from the taxman and a tax refund of £1,155.

In other words, he can buy a share in a property syndicate for £6,410 at a total personal cost of £3,845 (£5,000 minus his tax refund of £1,155). This means he buys all his syndicate shares/units each year at a 40% discount.

Otherwise the facts are exactly the same as in the previous examples: the property investments grow by 7% per year, rental profits are reinvested tax free, Gordon reinvests his higher-rate tax relief in an ISA, and annuities are used to generate pension income.

After 20 years Aaron will end up with a pension income of £24,091 whereas Gordon will end up with £38,780. Gordon has an impressive 61% more income than Aaron.

Conclusion

Investing in residential property through a self-invested personal pension could produce a far higher retirement income than investing in property directly.

It's quite possible that you will end up with two-thirds more income.

Looked at another way, by going the pension route you can possibly get away with saving much less than someone who invests outside a pension.

Either way, the fantastic tax reliefs available to pension savers will have an enormous impact on your ability to plan for your retirement.

Every property investor should consider investing in a pension fund when residential property joins the list of allowed investments in 2006.

Remember it doesn't have to be an all-or-nothing decision. Many property investors will probably invest in both to enjoy the best of both worlds: tax reliefs on their pension investments and free access to their directly-held property investments.

Chapter 7

Step-by-Step Action Plan

The new pension rules will only come into force on April 6th 2006. However, if you're interested in investing in property SIPPs there is plenty you should consider doing, and not doing, so that you are ready for A-Day.

The following is a short action list to help get you started.

Bear in mind that not all the pension changes are understood with 100% certainty. So be wary of taking action that you cannot undo!

Start a Commercial Property SIPP Now

If you've been looking into the possibility of investing in commercial property through a SIPP make sure you don't procrastinate for too long.

Come April 6th 2006 the borrowing limits for SIPPs will be drastically reduced and you may find your plans are scuppered somewhat.

From that date you will no longer be able to borrow 75% of the purchase price of the property. You'll only be able to borrow up to 50% of the value of your pension savings.

So if you only have £25,000 of pension savings you will be able to borrow £75,000 up to April 5th and only £12,500 after that.

But Don't Invest For Tax Reasons Only

I've met quite a few investors recently who are toying with the idea of investing in a commercial property SIPP even though they know nothing about commercial property. There's no doubt in my mind that they're attracted by the tax breaks more than the idea of investing in commercial property.

In my opinion this is a lousy strategy. If you don't know anything about commercial property, don't invest in a commercial property SIPP. Keep your powder dry until 2006 and you'll be able to get those same tax breaks by investing in residential property.

Furthermore, the problem with the current pension rules is that your SIPP cannot buy commercial property that you or your company currently own. This means your company would have to change premises if you wanted to own the property through a pension plan. This may cause tremendous upheaval. From 2006 this rule will be scrapped and buying your company's existing premises will be possible.

Set up a Stakeholder Pension or SIPP Now

Because the borrowing limits on residential property SIPPs will be quite stingy, the more money you can contribute now the better. Remember, from April 6th you will only be able to borrow 50% of your pension fund's net assets. So the more you can get in now the more you will be able to borrow come A-Day.

Of course you won't be able to invest in residential property straight away so if shares aren't your thing consider investing in low-risk assets such as cash and bonds.

One option would be to open a SIPP account with one of the existing providers that specialises in commercial property. For example, Suffolk Life has an entry-level SIPP with low charges provided you keep your money in cash. Another option would be to start contributing to a stakeholder pension. The charges are extremely low and no charges can be made for transferring out of the scheme to a SIPP at a later date.

Remember when doing this that there is no going back – once your money has been invested you cannot get it back again until you retire!

Consider Selling Property

One way of getting a cash lump sum into a SIPP after A-Day would be to sell existing assets and use your profits to make SIPP contributions. This is a more aggressive type of planning but something you should certainly bear in mind.

Example

Liz and Martin, a married couple, own a property worth £120,000 which they inherited a year ago when it was worth £105,000. It earns rental income of £8,400 per year. Martin is an out-of-work actor and Liz has a successful web design business and earns profits of £60,000 per year. It's 2006 and Liz would like to know what she stands to gain or lose by selling the property and investing the proceeds in a residential property SIPP.

Looking at the tax position, there will be no capital gains tax to pay when the property is sold because the £15,000 profit will be easily covered by Liz and Martin's combined capital gains tax exemptions.

Martin can then transfer his share of the proceeds to Liz because he doesn't have any earnings and therefore cannot contribute anything meaningful to a pension. Liz now has £120,000 to invest.

She decides to invest £40,000 per year over three years in a SIPP. This will earn her £33,846 in basic-rate tax relief and £12,261 in higher-rate relief. She'll now be able to buy a new property inside her SIPP and it will earn rental income that is completely tax free.

Setting up a SIPP will involve fees and selling and buying a new property will involve legal fees and possibly stamp duty. These costs will have to be balanced against the tax savings.

Make Sure You Stay Flexible

Your investment choices will be greatly increased after April 2006 so make sure you do not commit to actions now that you may later regret.

For example, you may want to think twice about investing in new property if you think you would be better served by a SIPP.

If you expect to receive a large lump sum between now and April 2006 remember that it may allow you to make a large pension contribution and claim a huge amount of tax relief if you have sufficient earnings.

Reconsider whether you should make Additional Voluntary Contributions. These are the top-up contributions that run in tandem with your employer's pension scheme. For many employees it is currently the only way they can make additional pension provision. From April 2006 you will be able to make your very own private pension provision. It could therefore be worthwhile stopping making these contributions now and saving the money. You'll be able to claim the full tax relief when you eventually invest the money in your own pension plan.

If you're planning to emigrate in the near future remember that pension tax reliefs are generally not available to non-residents.

Lastly, remember to be patient. It will take some time for the various SIPP providers and insurance companies to set up a range of competitive residential pension products.

Become Better Informed

Find out more about self-invested personal pensions by visiting the various SIPP providers' websites. Some of them contain a lot of useful information.

Consider investing in different *types* of property. For example, investigate the pros and cons of property syndicates. There's a lot of information available online. Property syndicates are likely to grow in popularity with pension investors.

High-yielding property (usually smaller properties that don't offer the same potential for capital growth) could also become particularly attractive. The rental income, currently taxed at rates as high as 40%, will be completely tax free inside a pension plan.

Company Pension Schemes

As a general rule, you should always stick with your current employer's pension scheme. The benefits are usually way too attractive to give up, especially if it's a final salary pension scheme.

However, you should certainly take advice about making a pension transfer from a previous employer's fund to a SIPP. This could be a useful way of building up pension savings that can be used to invest in property. This option is likely to appeal most to investors who are at least 10 years from retirement and who are skilled property investors.

Protect Yourself From the Lifetime Allowance

From April 2006 the maximum amount of money you can accumulate within a pension will be £1.5 million. If you think your pension savings will exceed this by then or even eventually, make sure you take steps to protect your existing entitlements. (See Chapter 5).

Chapter 8

The Tremendous Benefits of Real Estate Investment Trusts (REITs)

Imagine buying a spread of top-quality residential properties all over the country for just £100. Imagine owning them without all the hassle and responsibility of being a landlord. Imagine having an expert team negotiate great property deals and track down the latest 'property hotspots' on your behalf. And imagine them doing this without charging extortionate fees.

Imagine earning a combined return of 13% per year without any hassle. And imagine if these returns were completely tax free.

Imagine being able to sell your properties within minutes so that you can reinvest the cash in something else or simply sit back and enjoy the spoils.

Sound too good to be true? Well such an investment product may be hitting our shelves in the near future.

In the March 2004 Budget, the Chancellor announced that the Government was looking into a new type of investment vehicle called a Real Estate Investment Trust (also known as a REIT). The aim of REITs is to help address the shortage of housing in Britain and provide investors with an easy way to save that doesn't involve investing in high-risk stock market investments or mundane bank accounts.

The broad details were sketched out in the Budget and industry experts were invited to submit their ideas. The Government remains committed to introducing REITs in the near future and published further details in the March 2005 Budget.

It's important to stress at this stage that nobody's entirely sure what shape REITs will take. However, there's a fair amount of consensus on some of the major points. And if the Government takes on board all the expert advice it has been given, this new way of investing in residential property could revolutionize your property pension planning almost as much as SIPPs will.

In this chapter I will outline how REITs are likely to work and their advantages and drawbacks.

What is a Real Estate Investment Trust?

REITs will probably look a lot like unit trusts, which allow you to invest in a big spread of stock market investments for as little as £50 per month. In fact, they'll probably look a lot more like their close but lesser-known cousin, the investment trust.

Investment trusts are very similar to unit trusts except the trust itself is listed on the stock exchange. Investors buy and sell shares in the investment trust and the investment trust then buys and sell shares in lots of other companies.

It's a fantastic concept because for a small amount of money you can gain exposure to a large number of companies.

REITs are likely to work in much the same way. The fund will raise cash from investors by placing a share offering and these funds will be used to buy residential or commercial property.

These properties will then be rented out and the income will be paid out to you, the shareholder. Investors will be able to buy and sell shares in the REIT whenever they please.

Other likely characteristics of REITs will be the following:

- **The REIT itself will not pay any or much tax.** It's critical to their success that there is no double tax charge, in other words one tax bill paid by the fund and another tax bill paid by the investor. REIT profits will therefore be tax free but investors will have to pay tax on the income paid out.

- **Investors will pay tax just like ordinary property investors.** Distributions of rental profits will be taxed just like ordinary rental income, in other words at either 22% or 40% depending on your tax status. Distributions of profits from property development and other activities will be taxed as ordinary dividends.

- **REITs are not tax shelters.** It's important to stress that REITs will not be tax shelters in their own right. So if you invest in them directly you will be subject to tax on your profits. However, there's a very good chance the Government will let investors invest in them via a pension plan and maybe via ISAs too. If this happens we'll have the most fantastic way of investing in residential property: more tax efficient, easier, safer and cheaper than other forms of property investment.

- **Most of the income will have to be paid out.** The Government's advisers have recommended that 95% of income be paid out each year.

- **Capital gains may be tax free.** The trust will pay no corporation tax on capital gains from selling investment properties. Tax will, however, be payable on profits from property development. If any capital gains are distributed to investors they will be taxed as property income, in other words at either 22% or 40%.

- **REITs will not be allowed to borrow much money.** The Government hasn't decided how much REITs will be allowed to borrow to invest in property but has indicated that the amounts will be restricted. The more a REIT borrows the less rental profit it will have to distribute, and the less rental profit distributed the less tax collected by the Government! Having their borrowings curtailed will force the funds to raise further finance as and when they want to purchase more properties, thereby ensuring that they are subject to regular external scrutiny. It would, however, considerably increase the expense of raising funds if new issues of shares were needed regularly.

Although the REIT itself will not be able to borrow money, remember that the Government wants to tax REIT income just like other property income. This means there's a good chance that you will be able to borrow yourself to invest in REITs and claim the interest as a tax deduction. This could make them a fantastic alternative to conventional buy-to-let property investments.

- **Commercial and Residential REITs will be allowed.** UK REITs will be able to invest in any property type, in any part of the world.

- **REITs will be listed on the stock exchange.** The Government prefers the structure of a closed-end fund. It has considered open-ended investment companies (OEICs) and authorised unit trusts (AUTs), but these structures are open-ended which makes it difficult to use them for property investment since investors can withdraw their money at any time, for which purpose a substantial cash reserve would have to be maintained. The most likely structure, therefore, seems to be a form of company in which shares can be bought and sold, rather than a fund that buys back investors' interests.

The Advantages of Investing in REITs

Liquidity

One of the major drawbacks of investing in property is its lack of liquidity. Liquidity is simply the ease with which an asset can be converted into cash without incurring any penalty, such as a significantly lower price. Shares are extremely liquid because they can be sold in minutes; property is illiquid because it's usually weeks or months before you can get your hands on your money.

Liquidity isn't important to all investors, however it is essential if you want to move quickly to take advantage of new investment opportunities. REITs, because they are likely to be listed on the London Stock Exchange, will be extremely liquid investments.

Low Charges

Buying property can be an expensive business. First there are the legal fees, surveyor's fees, the letting agent's fees, maintenance fees and so on.

A big real estate investment trust will probably enjoy tremendous 'economies of scale' and hence the charges should be far lower than investing directly.

Lower Volatility than Shares

You can never get rid of risk completely but investment analysts find it easier to predict the earnings of something like a real estate investment trust, which earns mainly rental income from year to year, than for other companies. This means there are rarely the kind of surprises that can cause share prices to gyrate.

A High Dividend Yield

Experience from other countries shows that REITs are fantastic for income investors. Because they pay out most of their income they will provide an excellent means of supplementing a retirement income without all the hassle of being a landlord. And if you invest through a pension plan this income will be completely tax free.

No Borrowing Required

For some investors, having to borrow money to invest in property is a turn-off. Because buying a property outright is beyond most investors' budgets, it's necessary to get a buy-to-let mortgage. However, borrowing money makes property investment a far riskier business. What if interest rates rise and your rentals no longer cover the mortgage? How are you going to pay the mortgage if the property is empty? What if property prices crash and your borrowings end up being far larger than the property is worth? Some investors could do without this stress.

Real estate investment trusts will be ideal for this type of investor because they're likely to be made available to both small and large investors, which means you'll probably be able to invest in them for as little as £100 per month.

Transparent and Regulated

If real estate investment trusts are listed on the stock exchange this will create an excellent environment for investors to monitor the performance of their investment over time.

Share prices are printed daily in newspapers, for example, and are easily available on the internet.

Investment trust companies are governed by company law and stock exchange rules, as well as certain accounting and corporate governance standards. They also have boards of directors who are legally obliged to act in the interests of shareholders and to monitor investment performance and control costs on their behalf.

All this provides a lot of protection for investors. REITs would probably be subject to the same or similar rules if they are listed.

Geographic Spread

Your £100 per month will not just buy you a slice of one property. Instead, you will be able to invest in a whole portfolio of properties dotted all over the country. Owning a share in more than one property, especially if those properties have a wide geographic spread, significantly reduces the risk of investing in property.

According to research by the University of York, over half of landlords in this country invest locally. Although this is probably the logical thing to do it is not ideal when it comes to reducing certain types of risk.

Tax-planning Potential

It's important to stress that REITs will not be tax shelters in their own right. In other words, they will not enjoy the same tax breaks as ISAs. However, it is possible that investors will be able to shelter their profits by investing through a pension plan and maybe an ISA.

It will be cheaper and easier to invest in REITs through a pension plan than normal residential property.

REITs will also provide further tax-saving opportunities. The problem with property is you usually cannot sell it piece by piece with the result that a property that has generated significant gains will often result in a large capital gains tax bill.

REITs, however, like shares, will be easier to sell in small parcels allowing you to make maximum use of your annual capital gains tax exemption.

For example, let's say a married couple bought a flat just under three years ago and it has risen in value by £50,000. If they sell it they will be able to deduct their annual CGT exemptions totalling £17,000 leaving taxable profits of £33,000. The total tax bill could be as much as £13,200.

Let's say instead they made the same profit by investing in REITs. Because REITs will be denominated in small units it will be possible for the couple to sell their holding piece by piece. If they can sell one parcel just before the end of the tax year and another at the beginning of the next tax year they will be able to claim two annual exemptions each and reduce their tax bill to £6,400 – a saving of £6,800.

Less Time-consuming than Being a Landlord

One of the biggest drawbacks of property investment is the time commitment. First there's all the research you have to do to find suitable property. Then there's the buying process which can drag on and ultimately fail. Finally, once you're a landlord there's all the admin and related tasks that need performing... even if you do employ a letting agent.

Compare that with someone who just invests £500 a month in a Footsie tracker for 20 years. He may end up with less money at the end of the day but he'll have saved an enormous amount of time. That time can be spent working productively or simply enjoying yourself.

Real estate investment trusts too will not be as time-consuming to invest in. You will have to pick the right ones but beyond that there will be no further time commitment.

Easy Income Reinvestment

One of the problems with investing in property is that it is usually quite difficult to reinvest your rental profits. For example, say you earn a £2,000 rental profit from one of your properties. What are you going to do with it? It's too little money to buy a new property or even to put a deposit on a new property.

As we've seen in many of the examples throughout this guide, being able to reinvest your profits successfully can make a massive difference to your overall returns.

REIT investors will not have this problem. Because the minimum investment is likely to be extremely low it will be possible to reinvest your rental profits in new property immediately.

The Drawbacks of REITs

REITs are certainly no panacea for the various problems property investors face. They have quite a few drawbacks of their own:

More Volatile than Other Property Investments

REITs may be less volatile than shares but, because they'll probably be listed on the stock exchange, they will definitely be a lot more volatile than other property investments.

In other words, you could wake up one morning and the price of your shares/units will have fallen by 5% or more. However, experience from the US has shown that the prices of this type of investment do not fluctuate very much because their future earnings (rental income) are quite easy to predict.

Limited or Zero Gearing

It's likely that, unlike regular investors, REITs will not be allowed to borrow much to invest in property. This means they will not be able to benefit from the 'magic of gearing' (see Chapter 1).

However, this should not be too much of a drawback if investors themselves are allowed to borrow to invest. Furthermore, the fact that they will not be able to borrow may also make them more stable and less volatile investments.

It's factors such as badly managed borrowings that cause a company's share price to gyrate wildly.

Potential Tax Penalties

There are fears that when REITs make capital gains from selling property and distribute them to investors tax will be payable at the investors' marginal income tax rate.

This would be bad news because income is taxed much more heavily than capital gains. For example, at least £8,500 of your capital gains are tax free each year.

However it's unlikely that REITs will regularly distribute their capital profits. Instead the funds will be reinvested in new properties. Then when you ultimately come to sell your REIT shares you will be able to claim all the usual capital gains tax reliefs and allowances.

Discounts and Premiums

The problem with all stock market listed investment funds is they always trade at either a discount or a premium to the value of their underlying property assets. This is certainly the American experience. For example, very well-known property funds have been known to trade at a 35% premium to their net asset value, whereas other less well managed funds can trade at a 20% discount if there are concerns over growth in rental income.

Discounts are not an issue if they remain steady. However, if you invest in a fund that goes from trading at a 5% discount to a 20% discount you will instantly lose 15% of your money,

High Yields May Mean Low Growth

If 95% of the rental income has to be paid out the REIT will have less to reinvest to produce capital growth... and capital growth is taxed much more favourably than rental income.

This may be the case but the total returns from this type of investment could be extremely impressive if the experience of US REITs is repeated here.

According to Ralph Block, author of *Investing in REITs*, the US equivalent has delivered returns of 12.6% per year over a 20-year period.

That's a pretty impressive return.

150

Chapter 9

How to Earn Pension Tax Relief in Excess of 40%

It's a little-known fact that certain investors may be able to enjoy tax relief *in excess of 40%* when they make pension contributions. This will be possible if you make a sizeable pension contribution in the same tax year that you sell property or any other asset subject to capital gains tax.

This tax-planning opportunity will be of great interest to property investors who are thinking of selling existing properties so as to invest the proceeds in a property pension plan. But it will also be of interest to anyone thinking about selling property after April 6 2006 and wanting to know how to obtain the largest possible capital gains tax savings.

To understand why it is possible to earn tax relief in excess of 40%, you have to know a little bit about how capital gains tax is calculated when you sell property or other assets.

At its simplest, a capital gain is calculated by deducting the cost of the asset from the selling price. From this figure you can then deduct taper relief (if you've held the asset for more than three years) and your annual capital gains tax exemption (currently £8,500 per person). What's left is the taxable profit.

Now for the important bit. This taxable profit is then *added to your other income* and taxed at either 20% or 40% or a combination of both rates, depending on how much income you've earned during the tax year and the size of the taxable profit.

This is where making pension contributions comes in handy if you're a higher-rate taxpayer: pension contributions have the effect of extending your basic-rate tax band so that more of your income and capital gains are taxed at either 22% or 20% respectively.

If you have a salary of more than £37,295 in the current tax year you are a higher-rate taxpayer and will pay 40% tax on your capital gains. However, if you make a £5,000 pension contribution in the current tax year this will have the effect of extending your basic-rate tax band by £5,000. As a result you will now pay only 20% tax on the first £5,000 of your capital gains.

From April 2006 it will be possible to do this on a much larger scale because from that date it will be possible to make much larger pension contributions. So in future it is likely to pay to sell assets such as property and make large lump sum pension contributions in the *same tax year.*

To find out how much extra tax you may be able to save let's examine a detailed example. This has been generously provided by Edinburgh financial adviser CTFS Ltd, who first introduced me to the concept. The example is based on tax rates and allowances for the current 2005/2006 tax year because we don't yet know what tax rates will look like after A-Day.

Example

Richard earns a salary of £47,295. That number has been chosen because it means he has exactly £10,000 of salary which falls into the 40% tax bracket. Let's say he sells a property and, after deducting the various reliefs and exemptions, is left with a taxable capital gain of £30,000.

Assuming he makes no pension contributions his tax bill would be calculated as follows:

Tax on Salary		£
First £4,895		0
Lower rate band:	£2,090 @ 10%	209
Basic-rate band:	£30,310 @ 22%	6,668
Higher-rate band:	£10,000 @ 40%	4,000
Total income tax		10,877

Tax on Property Sale		£
Higher-rate band:	£30,000 @ 40%	12,000

Total income and capital gains tax   22,877

Because the level of Richard's salary ensures he is a higher-rate taxpayer his entire capital gain is taxed at 40%. But what if Richard makes a pension contribution of £30,000? This will extend his basic-rate tax band for the income tax and the capital gains tax calculation. His tax bill is then calculated as follows:

Tax on Salary		£
First £4,895		0
Lower rate band:	£2,090 @ 10%	209
Basic-rate band:	£30,310 @ 22%	6,668
Basic-rate band extension:	£10,000 @ 22%	2,200
Total income tax		**9,077**

Tax on Property Sale		
Balance of basic-rate band:	£20,000 @ 20%	4,000
Higher-rate band:	£10,000 @ 40%	4,000
Total capital gains tax		**8,000**

Total income and capital gains tax   17,077

The total tax saving is £5,800 (£22,877 - £17,077).

This tax saving comes about because Richard's basic-rate tax band is extended by the amount of the gross pension contribution, £30,000, which means that £10,000 of his salary and £20,000 of his capital gain is taxed at the basic rate.

Note use of the term 'gross pension contribution'. Richard's personal pension contribution in this example is £23,400 and the remaining £6,600 represents the taxman's top-up contribution (see Chapter 3).

So Richards total tax saving from making the pension contribution is:

	£
Income of £10,000 taxed at 22% not 40%	1,800
Capital gains of £20,000 taxed at 20% not 40%	4,000
Pension tax relief given at source	6,600
Total tax saving	**12,400**

His total tax saving expressed as a percentage of his pension contribution is:

$$12,400/30,000 \times 100 = 41.33\%$$

Summary

After A-Day it will be possible to carry out creative tax planning by making large lump sum pension contributions in the same tax year that you dispose of property or other assets subject to capital gains tax.

In some instances it will be possible to save tens of thousands of pounds in capital gains tax by following this technique.

Glossary

A-Day
April 6th 2006, the date residential property will be allowed as a pension investment. Other important pension changes, such as more generous contribution limits, will also be introduced from this date.

Additional Voluntary Contributions
Top-up pensions that allow members of occupational pension schemes to make additional pension contributions.

Alternatively Secured Income
The new and more flexible type of pension income that will be allowed as an alternative to buying an annuity when you reach age 75. Available to members of all pension schemes.

Annuity
An income purchased by investing a lump sum with an insurance company. The two main types are compulsory annuities and purchased annuities (see below).

Basic-rate relief
The tax relief paid straight into your pension pot by Inland Revenue. Calculated using the 22% basic rate of income tax. For example, if your contribution is £100 your gross contribution will be:

$$£100/0.78 = £128.21,$$

with £28.21 paid direct to your pension provider by the taxman.

Capital Gains Tax Exemption
Currently £8,500 per person, this is the amount allowed as a tax deduction from your profits from selling property, after deducting taper relief.

Compulsory Annuity

The pension for life that currently has to be bought with three-quarters of your pension savings when you reach age 75. The amount you earn will depend on your age, sex and the level of interest rates. This type of income is fully taxed.

Defined Benefit Scheme

Also known as a final salary pension scheme, your pension is dependent on your years of service and your final salary. For example, you may be entitled to 1/60th of your salary for each year you've worked for the company.

Defined Contribution Scheme

Also known as money purchase pension schemes, your employer promises to pay a 'defined contribution', eg 5% of your salary, into your pension fund. Your final pension then depends on how the pension fund's investments perform.

Higher-rate Tax

Currently 40%, it applies to all your income over £37,295.

Higher-rate Relief

The tax relief for contributions to pension schemes by higher-rate taxpayers. Claimed when you submit your tax return and calculated by multiplying your gross pension contribution by 18%. For example, let's say you contribute £100 to a pension plan. Your higher-rate tax relief is calculated as follows:

£100/0.78 = £128.21 x 18% = £23.08

Income Drawdown

The more flexible type of pension income that members of certain types of pension schemes, such as SIPPs, can take before reaching the age of 75. After A-Day income drawdown will become even more flexible.

Money Purchase Pension Scheme

See defined contribution pension schemes.

Occupational Pension Scheme

Company pension schemes, usually structured as final salary schemes but increasingly as money purchase schemes.

Personal Allowance

The first £4,895 of your income that is completely tax free.

Pension Transfer

The transfer of money from one pension scheme to another, for example from an old occupational scheme to a self-invested personal pension.

Purchased Annuity

The type of pension for life that anyone with a lump sum can acquire. Similar to compulsory annuities except you only pay tax on the interest portion of each annuity payment; the capital portion is completely tax free. Useful for people who need to maximize their retirement income.

Real Estate Investment Trusts

Also known as REITs, these are the new residential and commercial property investment vehicles that were announced in the 2004 Budget. They are to property what unit trusts and investment trusts are to shares. In other words, they will allow you to own a share in a big portfolio of residential and commercial property for a small outlay. Should be attractive for investors looking to maximize their income.

Self-invested Personal Pension

Also known as SIPPs, they're very similar to other personal pension schemes except they allow greater investment flexibility. For example, they can be used to invest in commercial property and from April 6th 2006 they will be available to residential property investors.

Taper Relief

Allowed as a deduction when calculating capital gains tax and ranges from 5% to 40%, depending on how long you have owned the asset.

Need Affordable & Expert Tax Planning Advice?

Try Our Unique Question & Answer Service

Taxcafe.co.uk has a unique online tax advice service that provides access to highly qualified tax professionals at an affordable rate.

No matter how complex your question, we will provide you with detailed tax planning guidance through this service. The cost is just £69.95.

To find out more go to **www.taxcafe.co.uk** and click the Tax Questions button.

Pay Less Tax!

... with help from Taxcafe's unique tax guides and software

All products available online at www.taxcafe.co.uk

- **How to Avoid Property Tax.** Essential reading for property investors who want to know all the tips and tricks to follow to pay less tax on their property profits.

- **Using a Property Company to Save Tax.** How to massively increase your profits by using a property company... plus all the traps to avoid.

- **Retire Rich with a Property Pension.** How to buy property at a 40% discount and completely avoid income tax and capital gains tax by using a personal pension plan.

- **How to Avoid Inheritance Tax.** A-Z of inheritance tax planning, with clear explanations & numerous examples. Covers simple & sophisticated tax planning.

- **How to Avoid Stamp Duty.** Little-known trade secrets that will help you reduce or eliminate the stamp duty bill when you buy property.

- **Non Resident & Offshore Tax Planning.** How to exploit non resident tax status to reduce your tax bill, plus advice on using offshore trusts and companies.

159

- ➤ **How to Avoid Tax on Your Stock Market Profits**. This guide contains detailed advice on how to pay less capital gains tax, income tax and inheritance tax on your stock market investments and dealings.

- ➤ **Incorporate & Save Tax.** Everything you need to know about the tax benefits of using a company to run your business.

- ➤ **Bonus vs Dividend**. Shows how shareholder/directors of companies can save thousands in tax by choosing the optimal mix of bonus and dividends.

- ➤ **Selling a Business**. A potential minefield with numerous traps to avoid but significant tax saving opportunities.

- ➤ **How to Claim Tax Credits.** Even families with higher incomes can make successful tax credit claims. This guide shows how much you can claim and how to go about it.

- ➤ **Property Capital Gains Tax Calculator**. Unique software that performs complex capital gains tax calculations in seconds.

Disclaimer

1. Please note that this Tax Guide is intended as general guidance only for individual readers and does NOT constitute accountancy, tax, investment or other professional advice. Taxcafe UK Limited accepts no responsibility or liability for loss which may arise from reliance on information contained in this Tax Guide.

2. Please note that tax legislation, the law and practices by government and regulatory authorities (eg Inland Revenue) are constantly changing and the information contained in this Tax Guide is only correct as at the date of publication. We therefore recommend that for accountancy, tax, investment or other professional advice, you consult a suitably qualified accountant, tax specialist, independent financial adviser, or other professional adviser. Please also note that your personal circumstances may vary from the general examples given in this Tax Guide and your professional adviser will be able to give specific advice based on your personal circumstances.

3. This Tax Guide covers UK taxation only and any references to "tax" or "taxation" in this Tax Guide, unless the contrary is expressly stated, refers to UK taxation only. Please note that references to the "UK" do not include the Channel Islands or the Isle of Man. Foreign tax implications are beyond the scope of this Tax Guide.

4. Whilst in an effort to be helpful, this Tax Guide may refer to general guidance on matters other than UK taxation. Taxcafe UK Limited does not accept any responsibility or liability for loss which may arise from reliance on such information contained in this Tax Guide.

Printed in the United Kingdom
by Lightning Source UK Ltd.
114748UKS00001B/114